BELIEVE

Also by the authors:

THE FARAWAY HORSES

BELIEVE
A Horseman's Journey

BUCK BRANNAMAN
AND WILLIAM REYNOLDS

THE LYONS PRESS
Guilford, Connecticut
An imprint of The Globe Pequot Press

The Lyons Press is an imprint of The Globe Pequot Press.

10   9   8   7

Printed in the United States of America

Designed by Maggie Peterson

ISBN 978-1-59228-899-1

The Library of Congress has previously cataloged an earlier (hardcover) edition as follows:

Brannaman, Buck.
    Believe : a horseman's journey / Buck Brannaman and Bill Reynolds.
        p. cm.
    ISBN 1-59228-433-7 (trade cloth)
    1.Horse trainers—United States—Anecdotes. 2. Horses—Training—United States—Anecdotes. 3. Horses—Behavior—United States—Anecdotes. 4. Human-animal communication—United States—Anecdotes. I. Reynolds, William, 1950- II. Title.

SF284.5.B73 2004
636.1_0835_092—dc22

                                                      2004059402

DEDICATION

In memory of two who mattered.
Of two who cared.
Of two who lived with grace.
Tom and Bill Dorrance

CONTENTS

ACKNOWLEDGMENTS

The acceptance and success of our first book, *The Faraway Horses,* was very exciting and gratifying for both Buck and me. *Believe* actually came about and was driven by the overwhelming interest of hundreds of people who wanted to share their stories with us and, ultimately, with you.

Thanks go to all these wonderful people who took the time—and had the courage—to share their success stories with us, including: Susan Alotrico, Amy Baker, Theresa Whitmarsh-Berryman, Don and Val Chase, Nicole Garcia, Laurie Gardos, Sherry Gulley, Barbara Jerviss, Shane and C. J. Jackson, Sissy Ledlow, Dianna McPhail, and Jean Palmieri.

We would also like to thank Donette Cowgill, Tyler Baldwin, and all the folks at The Lyons Press, especially Steve Price, Jay Cassell, Tony Lyons, Jane Reilly, and Kathryn Mennone.

As with *The Faraway Horses,* special thanks go to the two shining stars that illuminate our way, Mary Brannaman and Kristin Reynolds.

FOREWORD

In 1993, Buck Brannaman and I were sitting in a branding pen at a ranch near Nye, Montana. It was May, and I had just come from my brother-in-law's wedding the night before in LA. I finally arrived about two A.M., given all the various flights one must take to get to Montana from anywhere, it seems. It had been a hurried journey, and with little sleep the morning call to coffee at four A.M. seemed a cruel joke. With fresh horses, the branding crew jogged and crow-hopped off to the morning ritual of gathering for a spring branding. I had come to join friends for a yearly get-together to brand, this time at a friend's place, the Flying C Ranch outside of Columbus, Montana. It was really just an excuse to rope, to rope anything. Brannaman always said a bad day of roping beats a good day raking. I still don't quite follow that, but I do like to rope when I can.

While we were waiting outside the branding pen for our turn to rope, quiet seemed to descend upon us. The only sounds that spring morning were the settling cattle and the wind in the trees, high on the canyon rims above us. It was a permissive quiet—one that allowed the mind to move around freely, not bound by ordered memories, or thoughts at parade rest waiting to be called upon. I recalled my first meeting with Buck Brannaman some eight years earlier in 1985 at a horse event in Malibu, California. I remembered his easy way around horses, and his shyness around the folks who were watching. He silently went about his business helping the young horses lose their fears and resistance. It was quite a sight; the wonder of simple action rewarded, of kindness given and trust received. I saw Buck in this situation again and again over the years. A few years later at a clinic in Colorado, I noticed that he still moved easily around the horses, but he had become more confident with the spectators. When answering their questions and responding to their comments, he seemed to be more aware of their concerns and how their concerns fit with their horses' problems. Buck left them with more tools to use than when they came, and his understanding even more appreciated. The rewards for all even greater. He seemed to hold them in his hands as moved around the little pen, working a new horse. Those watching were starting to see the horse—and themselves—through his eyes. A greater understanding for both horse and rider. More, it was apparent, was in store for this young man.

Lap dissolve: New York City:
In 1998, Buck and I found ourselves sitting together in a tiny hotel room in New York City with video cameras and microphones, as Buck was being interviewed by the working Hollywood press. A writer named Nick Evans had spent a little time traveling with Buck in the mid-1990s, and had framed his book's main character, Tom Booker, around him. No one figured it would amount to anything, but that book became a best-seller and was the basis for the very successful Robert Redford movie, *The Horse Whisperer.* Buck and I had

been involved in helping to make the film, but standing in that little branding pen in Nye, Montana, back in 1993, neither Buck nor I could have ever imagined that what Buck did for a living would have such an impact on so many people. Let alone that Buck himself would be the model for a screen hero played by a star like Robert Redford. Not Buck. He was definitely something special, but just with horses—right?

It turned out that Buck was something special at many things, once you really got to know him. Unfortunately, getting to know him can be a tough undertaking, as he is constantly on the move. Getting a real grip on Buck is kind of like trying to capture mercury on the deck of a moving ship. A tough deal. The thing about Buck is, good things always seem to happen to him. "Brannaman Luck," it's been called. For the twenty-odd years I have known him, more good things have happened to Brannaman than bad. And in fact, the good things have way outnumbered the bad—especially as time went on. Why? Because as he has evolved, he has aimed himself at life in a positive way. As he removed resistance in his own life, he has done the same in the horses he has worked with, and with that, has managed to remove resistance in "their" humans as well. The result? Everybody won. Including Buck. He found people cared more and more, and the feelings they had for their horses' successes stuck. Stuck to the point that when they went home, they found they listened more and empathized more with their family members, their spouses, their friends . . . everyone. Everybody won. But don't misunderstand; Buck's had his share of trouble, starting when he was just a kid in Idaho. He had a horrible childhood, one that eventually led to placement in a foster home with exposure to horses—something that ultimately saved his life.

Brannaman Luck? Maybe. Certainly, the more than ten thousand horses he has started are better off, and more importantly, the people he has touched through their horses are better off, as well. They seemed to take quickly to his approach of working on an equal relationship, from a place of mutual respect and understanding. It really works. Probably would work at the United Nations, if we could get them to give it a try.

In 2001, Buck and I released his own story, *The Faraway Horses*. It was a hard story for him to work on, and we had many sleepless nights of rewrites and loud discussions, but it ultimately hit a chord with readers. People seemed to enjoy and identify with this young man's quest to better not only his own life, but the lives of all the horses he encountered in his travels. The interesting thing is, he touched as many, if not more, people in the process.

Believe is about some of those people Buck has met, and their own personal journeys to success. It's about the new paths they started down after meeting Buck in the center of some corral somewhere, standing next to a quivery young horse. The stories contained in this book are really about what happened to these people after they'd met Buck, and he had moved on—what they did with what he gave them, and how they are better for having met him.

This book is for everyone, horse owners and non-horse owners alike. It's for people who know which end of a horse to feed as much as it is for people who don't have any interest in horses at all. This book is about hope and about finding life's satisfaction in the journey, no matter where you're headed. It's about taking the time to treat each relationship we encounter or initiate with care. It's about understanding and courtesy, elements that can make the clouds part and the sun shine.

In a nutshell, that's what Brannaman does with horses; he gives them his time and his attention, which brings clarity to the thoughts and actions of both horse and rider. This giving of attention, of serious consideration, is something we need to do more of in our day-to-day lives. I have seen the results myself, and it is truly life-altering—for both parties in the relationship.

We are all in this world together. And with people like Buck Brannaman sharing his way with us, we are all better off. *Believe.*

William Reynolds
Santa Ynez, California
2004

INTRODUCTION

It would have been about mid-morning on that winter day in 1968, in Coeur d'Alene, Idaho. There had been a wet snow— not much of it, but the kind that has so much moisture in it that everything is frigid, right down to the core of every rock, tree, and miserable warm-blooded creature. It was the kind of cold that takes all night to shake off, and by that time you have to go out and brave it again.

On this one cold day, a little boy walked out the door of his house to do his morning chores. As he did every morning, he found himself fighting mightily with about three hundred feet of half-frozen garden hose. There were no outdoor water lines; in order to fill the water tanks for the family's livestock, an enormous hose from the side of the house had to be drawn out for use and then coiled up again.

The horses would cluster around the boy as the seemingly endless stream dribbled from the crunchy hose. After watering the horses, the kid manhandled the hose across the yard to water a handful of small-bagged, pitifully poor milk cows, standing at the ready, mooing and grunting for his attention. Every morning, the water had to flow, frozen hose or not—even if it meant he had to beat the hose with a hammer. Every morning before he went off to school, that kid knew what was ahead of him.

Meanwhile, an older boy—the little kid's older brother— would head toward the huge milking barn where his own

chores awaited him. (Seen through adult eyes, he would be surprised to realize that the family's huge milking barn was actually
only slightly bigger than a one-car garage.) The older boy would
swing his milk cans to urge the cows into their stanchions, anxious to get through the morning milking. As he worked, he
would occasionally glance through the barn doors to see the
hose lurching past, or watch as it got hung up on the basement
windowsill. This would invariably be followed by great invisible
tugging and whipping about of the hose, accompanied by muf-
fled grunts and curses from his younger brother. The kid was a
pretty sensitive youngster, but nevertheless became quite accomplished at swearing, especially when the hose wouldn't co-
operate - something that happened roughly every fifty feet or so
that he tried to drag the darned thing.

While slow in coming, success was eventually achieved,
and the kid would finally get the hose out to the last water
tank and the water would begin to trickle out of the hose
and he would wait and wait and wait. Just standing there
waiting, shaking and shivering in the snowy, cold air, waiting for the water tank to fill up. Well, like any six- or seven-
year-old would, he'd get a little bored and would start
looking around, inspecting and exploring. On this particular
day, he looked up at the far end of the meadow at this Pon-
derosa pine tree that was sort of two trees in one. It had a
deep cleft in it, about three feet off the ground. He saw
something in the cleft of that tree, and really thought he
should investigate. After all, he did have a little time while
waiting on that water tank to fill up. And even though he
could have perhaps walked on over to the milking shed to

assist his older brother, he was sure that his brother would get along fine without him.

Adventure seemed more important at this point, and he walked to the end of the meadow to investigate this thing in the cleft of the great pine tree. It had snow all over it, so he looked underneath the snow to find a tiny flicker. Now, a flicker is a woodpecker-type of bird found in the northern parts of the United States. The flicker may be found all over, and there were certainly plenty of them around the area in the summertime, but this was the middle of the winter. You didn't often see birds in the wintertime, not like this.

The bird was obviously very cold and very sick. The boy thought he'd bring the bird to the house, hoping his dad wouldn't think it a waste of time and fall into such a foul mood that he wouldn't let him warm up the bird. He picked up the poor, frozen thing, and as he did, the bird, which seemed more dead than alive, let out a horrific *squawk* and flapped its wings. Naturally, this surprised and terrified the boy, and he dropped the frantic creature to the ground. His immediate instinct was to strike back at the thing that had so startled him, and without thinking, he stepped on the bird and killed it. He instantly realized his error—that in spite of his good intentions to save a sick creature, his instincts had caused him to kill it. He stood there quite a while, thinking about what he had done, thinking about actions versus reactions, and the shame poured over him, just as the water started to spill from the overfilled stock tank in the distance.

That moment stayed with the little boy, and it would continue to bother him his whole life. As an adult, he often thought back to that cold morning in Idaho and wonder what it was that made him kill something he was trying to help. He never really forgave himself, even though he knew in his heart that the act wasn't calculated or premeditated or intentional. He believes his immediate instinct to protect himself from that bird at all costs may have been based on his never-ending fear of his father—someone he and his brother felt the need to protect themselves from every day of their young lives.

When asked years later if he could remember something pleasant or good about his father, he thought and thought and said, "No; I was never not afraid of the man." That fear, the fear that lived within the boy and his older brother, might well have been what motivated the boy to act so instinctively to kill the bird he believed would hurt him. Who knows? This isn't about blame. But just like the flicker in the snow, growing up in his father's house stayed with the boy, and he never stopped feeling great distress and concern whenever he came across something that was living in fear and despair. The man that boy has become believes that his encounters with fear at an early age led him to spend his life trying to erase the fear and lessen the despair of those around him, be they man or beast.

I don't believe what happened between the boy and the bird happened by accident. I'm sure some would find it strange that such a small, insignificant event would mean anything at all to a person like me, all these years later, all these miles down the road. But it does, of course. I was that little boy.

I've had a lot of ups and downs in my life. Many of those

who read my first book, *The Faraway Horses,* know a bit about my history, and have become a part of my present and my future in a way I never would have thought possible. I've been blessed with an ability to explain and share an understanding of fear and how to find a way to live beyond it with thousands of people over the years. Complete strangers have been able to recognize and find that special place with me and then create it in their own lives. This doesn't happen with every acquaintance, but often enough that the phenomenon is hard to explain, otherwise.

The message of this book isn't really about despair or trouble. It's about winning a victory over the many burdens in our lives. Do any of us ever really win? Well, I don't know. I don't think so. But we can each gain a little bit of ground, every day of our lives. Hopefully, you gain enough ground that, if you're walking the right path, lots of little victories appear along the way. There will always be heartaches and despair to deal with, but it's how we deal with them that really shapes us as individuals, and determines what kind of an influence we're going to have on those around us. And isn't that really what it's all about?

Horses don't care what color you are, how tall or short or how small or large you are, or whether you're rich or poor, attractive or unattractive. None of that means anything to the horse. A horse takes you at face value for how you make him feel at that moment. It seems to me this would be a good way for all of us people to behave with each other, too. Lord knows, in this day and age, the whole world could stand a bit more of that.

I hope you enjoy this book, and I hope it helps you to enjoy your own life's path. Just by reading this, you've already made me a part of your journey, and I'd like to thank you for your faith, and assure you that even a rough trail can smooth out. If you do nothing else, believe.

Buck Brannaman
Sheridan, Wyoming
2004

BELIEVE

CHAPTER 1

COPING WITH FEAR

Fear is something that I deal with a lot in my work with horses. It can be so overwhelming that it permeates your entire life. It can make you say and do things you wouldn't dream of doing any other time. Sometimes when a person is afraid or intimidated, they will be a little defensive toward others, or they may be rude or aggressive. Often, they're just putting up a wall, trying to protect themselves from some unknown fear.

Early on, when I first started working with people, I would see the symptoms of a person who lived a life in constant fear. The symptoms were different for each individual. Some were very timid and withdrawn; others could be quite aggressive. With fear comes other issues, including low self-esteem and doubting yourself. I've found that frightened horse owners often can overcome their fear of doing the wrong thing by doing something else that is safe. Just be proactive and do *something*. Don't be locked up by fear. So many times, people fear situations where they believe they have no control. Of course, you can't play God with everything around you, but many times you can shape what's happening in a way that eliminates whatever it is that's frightening you.

Horses can be scary animals to work with because of their size and apparent skittishness, but often fear of an animal is just covering up other personal issues that the person is trying to deal with. I've never seen a situation where a person was just simply afraid of their horse, and didn't have that same characteristic fear permeating the fabric of their entire life. It always does. I guess because horses are larger and more powerful than we are, working with them can be a very revealing time for the owner—any fear that was there to start with is greatly magnified. And I don't know anyone who wants the things below the surface of their psyches to be revealed publicly. Surprise! Around horses, it all comes to the surface.

Over the years, I've found that some folks are intimidated by me. Although I often have to use a microphone at my clinics so everyone can hear, my natural speaking voice is already fairly loud. I've also been doing this for about a hundred years, and know just about everybody out there in the horse world, so I've got a little celebrity. All of this added to people's expectations creates some fear and intimidation inside them. I know that this job comes with a big responsibility to do my best to put my students at ease, while making sure I teach them and work with them to understand and accomplish the various things they have come to learn. But I am also there to help them take a look inside—to see what they need to do to help themselves, not just their horses.

When I was a little boy I dealt with fear every day, living with my father. He was a tough guy with a severe drinking problem, which gave him cause to be pretty miserable. I know he was miserable because he often took it out on me and my older brother, Smokie. I was afraid of being hurt, and that fear of pain is an amazing force that's very hard to shake off. So, because fear is fear, whether you have two legs or four, fear for a horse can be just as terrifying and petrifying as it can be for humans. The reactions may be different, but it's still fear speaking.

This brings me to a little hitch in the trail that might mean something to many of you.

A couple of years ago, while buying supplies at a ranch wholesaler in Billings, Montana, I met a girl who recognized my name from *The Faraway Horses* and *The Horse Whisperer*. We started talking and she said, "I don't know if you remember my dad. He lived across the fence from you in Whitehall, Montana." I did remember her dad, and immediately, my mind went back to something that I hadn't thought of in quite a while. The pages of my memory just fell open.

One day, my brother and I had just come home from school when we both realized we had neglected a chore. I was ten years old, and understand that youngsters can easily forget things—especially now, as I have a ten-year-old daughter. My brother and I had a lot of chores, a lot of responsibility—more than most kids that age should probably have—and somewhere along the way, we had left a gate open and one of our geldings had gotten in with others in an adjacent corral. It was no big deal, they were happy as clams, but it made my dad angry and he was hollering at us like we'd set the place on fire. I was dreading what was going to happen next, because you never got through one of those deals without a whipping. My dad never just told you what you'd done wrong and moved on. True to form he marched us outside into the yard and had us grab hold of a pole fence next to our back door. He then proceeded to whip us across the back and legs with an eight-foot stock whip about as long as a fly rod.

I remember how it felt walking from the back steps over to that rail fence. The overwhelming fear of what was coming was more overpowering than having the whip cut my shirt off my back. I remember that while he was whipping me, I looked across about three-eighths of a mile to the ranch next door. There was that girl's father, watching the two of us get whipped. It was quite a distance away, but I swear I looked right into his eyes from there. And I swear he looked right into mine. Maybe he couldn't really see what was going on, but I think he could, and he didn't come help or try to stop what was happening. I can't imagine, all these years later, being an adult and doing nothing while watching something like that. I just can't believe that he didn't realize what was going on, that he didn't hear the pop and snap of the whip and my brother's and my cries.

But in his defense, my dad was a very violent, dangerous man. Had this neighbor come over, my dad might very easily have shot him. So it was just one of the many whippings we got in our lives. We survived that one. I look back and I think that it was probably okay that the man didn't come over. And Smokie and I knew that if we had run, it would have been even worse for us when my dad finally caught us. So we stayed.

My point in telling this story is to illustrate that I've seen paralyzing fear from a very personal perspective, and I also understand it from an outsider's view. I know the kind of fear Sherry relates in her story, and I can't help but feel for the folks who make their way into my clinics who are just as scared as I was that day my daddy whipped me.

I also tell this story to encourage others to intervene and to help those who are paralyzed by their fear—or at risk of being embarrassed by it—because embarrassment often increases the power of that fear. It's very important to realize that many of those who are stuck in place by their fear may very well be doing the best they can with what they have, and it's up to us to understand where they are coming from. You have to put yourself in someone else's shoes before you can really appreciate why and how they will react to outside influences or situations. This counts for people as well as horses.

I do the best I can to try to eliminate the fear that paralyzes riders and their horses. Sometimes just a small act of kindness is all you need to get started. Kindness is contagious. When shown genuine kindness, many folks will find sureness and confidence growing within them. This leads to being more certain of where you want to go in life and how to get there, which is in itself a very empowering thing. I believe that kindness and patience and faith are more powerful than negativity. In fact, I'm sure of it, because I've seen it work with humans and animals alike.

When Sherry mentions in her story that she had been in several wrecks, she means she had either fallen off, been bucked off, or had been scared so badly that she found herself reacting to her animal in a fearful way. Sometimes it's simply a matter of the rider's own fear; the horse is actually doing everything just right.

Sherry mentions attending one of my ranch-roping clinics, which are designed to teach folks how to handle sick cattle out on the range when it isn't practical to run them for miles into a corral or pen for doctoring. I teach my students how to throw their ropes around a calf's neck and around his hind feet, to immobilize him. This enables them to capture the animal so that medicine or treatment can be administered quickly. Sherry had a hard time with the roping, but I think she learned an even greater lesson that day. She saw that taking a moment to offer help to someone in need can make a great difference for just about everyone involved.

Sherry also refers to her horse as being a good babysitter. That's pretty self-explanatory—a horse that's solid and gentle will take care of her. When I worked with Sherry in the ring and asked her to move a little faster with her horse than she was comfortable with, it created an increase in tension for her; it brought her back to that fear of being bucked off or run away with, even though she knew her horse was dependable and solid. In a clinic environment, it's important to ask riders to get out of their comfort zone, to move into an area that's unfamiliar to them. On an emotional level, I'm holding their hands until they gain the confidence to believe they're going to survive on their own. You have to care about what you're doing, but first you have to care about the people you're doing it with.

A friend once told me, "They don't care how much you know until they know how much you care." I think that's true for human beings and for horses alike. I was visiting with a dear friend of mine a few years ago, and she said, "You know, after you're dead and gone, there's going to be a lot of people who remember you not so much for being a great horseman, but for how you made them feel when you were around them." I've mentioned that to other people over the years—horse people, plumbers, electricians, pool boys, whatever—and they agree. People really do remember how you make them feel. And that's something that a lot of folks don't put much effort into these days.

Over the years of working with horses and their people, I've found many truths in nature that also apply to human beings. As I said before, horses don't care if your skin is dark or light, if you're tall or short, whether you have nice teeth or no teeth at all; it just doesn't matter to them. What does matter is how you make them feel, and they will respond positively if you treat them with respect, patience, and understanding.

Sherry learned firsthand that my responding positively toward her helped her overcome her fears. She learned that responding positively toward her horse improved their relationship dramatically. She also saw the benefits of quietly offering a helping hand to those in need. I'm happy to have had a small part in her discoveries.

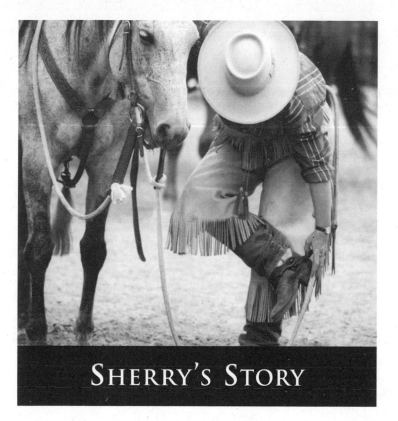

SHERRY'S STORY

In 1994, I was a middle-aged screenwriter on a green horse. It was a typical situation that many women seem to find themselves in: I'd enjoyed riding rent-by-the-hour horses as a child, and in my late thirties, I finally decided to get my own horse and ride again. Soon after buying a three-year-old gelding, I realized I needed help. Oh, I had a good horse. I was the one who needed to be trained!

I observed Buck at one of his clinics in 1995, and rode in one for the first time in 1996. It seemed to me that Buck always told it like it was, which was both good and bad. The people who really wanted to learn were able to accept Buck's no-nonsense instructions and observations, while others seemed to be offended when Buck didn't automatically compliment them.

I belonged to the first group; I was there to learn. I was out of bounds and out of control on my gelding. I didn't even know what a canter lead was, much less know how to ask for the correct one. I'd experienced quite a few wrecks and was a bit scared. My horse was a good babysitter, but he was green and couldn't do much to improve my balance and riding ability for me.

When we were asked at the end of the day if we had any questions, I told Buck I thought I had a really good horse, but I felt myself constantly fighting fear, which caused many problems when riding. For example, I would lean forward and keep a death grip on the reins, clenching my legs against my horse and just hoping everything would be okay. I'd reached the point where even getting on my horse caused my stomach to ache.

Buck said something so simple and profound: He told me to replace my fear with knowledge. I realized how wise his suggestion was; if I could know what to do and what to expect, I would be safe and stop being so fearful.

The concept of replacing fear with knowledge works for me throughout every aspect of my life, whether it's applied to everyday choices and decisions or to larger issues like beginning something I haven't done before. Any time I am unsure and lack confidence, I make a point of becoming more knowledgeable about the task. I ask questions, do my research, and learn. This doesn't always result in everything going smoothly, but it does allow me to be more prepared.

It took a lot of thought and help from friends and instructors, but over the years I've learned how to truly ride a horse. I know how they think, learn, and communicate. I know how to help and support them through difficult situations. My horses look to me for guidance and support rather than wondering what's going on with the crazy woman riding them.

I now know what a lead is and how to ask for the correct one. I'm still riding green horses, only now they don't have to babysit me. I've continued to ride in Buck's clinics whenever I can, and I've learned many things about horsemanship from him. I've also observed great humanitarian acts.

A few years ago I rode my young mare in one of Buck's ranch-roping clinics. My farrier happened to be there and observed me in action. The next time he came to shoe my horses, he began teasing me about my performance at the clinic and how impressed he was with my skill at roping myself and my horse's head—but wasn't I supposed to rope the cow?

After the teasing, he grew serious and said, "That Buck Brannaman did a really neat thing for a friend of mine." He went on to say that the quiet fellow I'd seen in a clinic the year before was a good friend of his. It seemed this man was starting a colt the summer after the roping clinic, and while he was out in the pasture, something spooked the colt. The rider was doing all the right things, and the colt began to settle down when they ran out of room and hit the hot-wire fence.

This was too much for the colt. He began to buck hard. The man was thrown and landed on the fence, where it's thought the horse kicked him as it leapt away. The man was hospitalized with a severe head injury, and after quite a long hospital stay and with much healing yet to do, the man went home to recuperate. He wrote a letter to Buck telling him the story. To his amazement, Buck wrote a very nice letter back, wishing him the best for a full recovery and offering as much encouragement as he could. The man was so touched and honored by Buck's kindness that he carefully folded the letter and carries it in his billfold to this day. That's how my farrier knew of Buck's kindness; his friend had carefully opened up the letter and shown it to him.

My farrier is a rough, tough, strong man, who grew teary-eyed when he told me the story. There was no way for Buck to have known what a huge impact his letter would make; it isn't often in this life that we get to see the huge result from such a seemingly small effort.

At the roping clinic where I kept roping myself, Buck asked some of the better hands to head calves so the rest of us could practice throwing loops at their heels. One of the fellows that had a calf necked is a great hand, but he has very poor vision. When calves are necked, after a few minutes they will stand quietly while the heel shots are thrown. The roper holding the calf is told to allow slack in the rope so the calf is not under any stress, as long as it stands still. The calf should not be allowed to step over the rope, however.

The arena's lighting was not bright, and this roper with

poor eyesight couldn't see how far off the ground his rope was. The calf stepped over it. Buck offered some friendly ribbing and then helped the calf get untangled. Everything was good-natured and friendly and continued on as before. A short time later, the same thing happened again. I knew the roper would be embarrassed that he had made the same mistake again, even though it was due to his impaired vision.

After I was able to quietly advise Buck of the situation, Buck quietly and with obvious respect made his move with such subtlety that no one but me realized what he did. He rode over near the roper and calf and turned his horse's hindquarters to the calf. As he was making comments to the riders he was facing, he purposely moved the hindquarters of his horse toward the calf to encourage the calf to step over the rope.

The legendary trainer Tom Dorrance always said, "It's the little things that make the difference." Buck is a prime example of that. He does so many wonderful little things— making positive observations, answering a simple letter that didn't require a reply, using his knowledge and finesse to help someone without making it obvious to others. Many people accomplish heroic deeds that make the headlines, but Buck Brannaman is heroic just in the way he carries out his life.

How does that affect me? I try to be more like Buck. I try to replace fear with knowledge. I help out when I can. I encourage, I smile, and I am dependable. I know the value of anonymously helping others who need a hand. I gain knowledge and I share it. I don't want to be Buck, but I will use his example to improve myself.

CHAPTER 2

QUALITIES FOR SUCCESS

Reading through the stories that my friends and students
have presented for this book, I think of the different human
and psychological characteristics these folks are discovering
about themselves, and then working on. What's interesting is
that so many folks take a lesson about working with a horse
and turn it into a lesson for themselves. Many don't even realize they have inner troubles to work out, but working with
horses always seems to bring those personal issues into focus
for them.

Recently, I was thinking about the things that are important in making a person a good horseman and that are also necessary in a good companion or friend, someone real desirable

to be around. I came up with eight characteristics or qualities that horses have and humans should emulate:

1. **Intuition.** Intuition is a gut feeling about something intangible, an unspoken sensitivity to what you're dealing with. As a result of evolution, horses and other animals have a natural ability to sense the emotional state of people and horses around them. In fact, they seem to have instinctual gut feelings about everything they come across. Unfortunately, people often don't listen to their inner voices the way animals do. I think it's very important to be open to your instincts, because it helps you get in touch with things that aren't on the surface. Whether men like to admit it or not, women seem to have quite a bit more of this instinctual inner knowledge, although I believe men can acquire it. I often joke that "A man can acquire intuition if he listens to his wife long enough," but it's really more than that. Human intuition is having the ability to look ahead and clearly see things in a very objective way. Everyone has a little of it, but I think women have a teaspoon more of it than men.

2. **Sensitivity.** I'm talking about emotional sensitivity. Horses are very intelligent creatures, and emotional sensitivity is something that all intelligent, thinking creatures possess. Everything around us can impact us and our horses emotionally in some way. If we are sensitive and observant of our horse's emotions, we can better anticipate and respond to their movements and actions. The same is true of humans:

If we are sensitive to our own emotions and those of people around us, we can better anticipate and respond to whatever comes our way. Now again, this is something that tends to be more true of women. The female of any species tends to be a little more sensitive and nurturing than the male, which generally holds true for human beings as well; women are generally more emotionally sensitive than men. There are men who are plenty sensitive, but it's not as widespread a characteristic among males.

3. **Change.** This is the ability to back up, back down, and change course if necessary, as opposed to beating your head against a wall and doing the same old thing, hoping that this time it might turn out differently. Horses take each new thing as it comes, and they're bright enough to think through a given situation. If a situation requires the horse to take a different course, he will, and that's what has helped keep horses alive through the ages.

We humans can be a stubborn bunch. If someone is going to back down and change course, it's usually the woman and not the man. Women seem to be better able to change their minds about things, while men tend to get stuck on one idea and insist on staying there, come hell or high water. Men are also more inclined to be steadfast in their beliefs, even when their beliefs turn out to be wrong or foolish. Change just seems like one more of those things that women are better at. Now, I know some men out there who have been married fifteen or twenty years, and would argue that women lose the ability to change as they grow older, but let's be honest: If you've ever been lost while driving in a big, confusing city with your wife, you know that she is more willing to change course (or stop and ask directions) than you are. This just seems to be the male nature.

The important thing to remember is that the ability to adjust your actions or outlook to fit whatever situation comes along is a great asset. Showing humility, respect, and lack of ego is not only a very pleasant and effective thing for people; horses react positively to it, too.

4. **Presence.** "Presence" means the feeling that flows off of any person who humbly but truly believes in himself and his abilities; someone at peace with himself and his environment. It's not about superiority or intimidation or aggression; presence is about being confident and at peace with yourself and your life. A healthy, well-treated horse exudes this self-confident, calm, sure presence, just like a healthy, well-treated human does.

5. **A nonaggressive attitude.** Be assertive, but not arrogant or demanding. Don't be a butthead. Focus on your goal and work toward stepping with care, but stepping forward always. No horse or man ever got very far being a jerk.

6. **Determination.** This is the ability to stick to something through thick and thin. Even when things

get very difficult, determination is the ability to stay on course. It's one of those very individual qualities. Some folks just have that inner core of determination that helps them push on, even when the odds seem their worst, even when it seems they have no chance of succeeding. I'm going to say one thing now, and I want you all to think about it: the racehorse Smarty Jones.

7. **Humility.** The concept of humility is so important, I'd underline it as being pivotal to a person's success or failure in the world. Humility is the ability to listen to and really hear what is being said, regardless of status or standing. That almost needs no explanation, but the following three words sum up how to gain this quality: observe, remember, and compare. *Observe* what is taking place, whether with man or beast; *remember* what you've done to cause others to make a certain decision or take a certain action; and *compare* the results of your actions this time around with the results of actions you may have taken in the past. Which outcome was better? Learn from it. If you can observe, remember, and compare effectively, and then have the ability to change course based on the outcome of what you've done, you will map out your course for success.

8. **Love.** Love is a complete and powerful thing. It includes the ability to love without being a victim. Sometimes loving can end up being an excuse for being victimized, taken advantage of, pushed around. But you can still have a huge capacity for love without being a victim or being taken advantage of.

These eight characteristics found in horses are also things that all of the wonderful people in this book are working on at one level or another. Now, just for the sake of comparison, I'm going to go back through the list and describe to you the kind of person that would probably never, ever get along with horses, or get along—period.

1. **Lack of intuition.** People who have no insight or ability to see beyond their own needs or wants. They have an expectation that what is on the surface is all there is to see.

2. **Lack of sensitivity.** Those who lack the ability or the confidence to feel or understand anything that isn't in their immediate sphere of existence; a lack of compassion for others.

3. **Stiff.** Stiff people make up their mind that they're going to do something a certain way and regardless of the results, they continue to do it that particular way—even if it doesn't work—because their pride makes them unable to back down or change course. This will guarantee failure every time.

4. **Over-presence.** I spoke of the almost magical presence of a person who is peaceful, self-confident, and completely at ease in his environment. At the other end of this spectrum are people who project a powerful, unconquerable presence, believing that their inner might will make them right.

5. **An aggressive attitude.** Some folks go beyond projecting power, and begin to exhibit it. This sort of threatening behavior often backfires because the natural

reaction to this is a feeling of extreme danger. Folks don't generally respond well to threats. Nor do horses.

6. **Lack of determination.** Obviously, people who don't put their back into it, don't get much out of it, whatever it might be.

7. **Lack of humility.** We've all met people who spend an entire conversation thinking about the importance of what they're going to say, and then trampling all over us to say it. You can actually see their minds working, thinking feverishly about how to drag the conversation back to them and what they think about everything under the sun. How can people who will not listen teach? Furthermore, how can they learn if all they hear is themselves?

8. **Anger and hatred.** Those who cannot love often believe the only way to avoid being hurt is to hurt others first. Victimize or be victimized.

It's pretty easy to sort out what kind of a person you'd rather be in the same room with. It's just as easy for horses to figure out what kind of person they can learn from. Theresa's story made me think of the things that horses and people have in common, and how we all learn best if taught with patience, humility, and understanding.

Theresa learned the importance of the items I've listed here in working with her troubled mare. Together, they had reached a point where they were both in a life-threatening situation, and had come to me for help. Unfortunately, this is the state many of my students are in when they arrive at my clinics—they're scared, worried, intimidated, and confused, at the end of their ropes. Fortunately, with a lot of hard work and dedication, these dangerous relationships between human and horse can be repaired.

In Theresa's case, she learned some wonderful lessons to help improve her relationship with her horses. One thing she speaks of is the importance of getting her horse to yield to her. Yielding is not about submission. It's more a matter of showing respect for one another. Think of it this way: you're waiting for a bus, and when it comes, several people push forward, refusing to yield to the others around them. This creates a negative feeling about the pushy people and leaves us with a situation where nobody gets anywhere. Then, consider someone who gives up his or her seat on a crowded bus; that person is showing consideration and respect without having been forced into it at all. That selfless, respectful sort of yielding is the kind of thing we should all strive for, with both humans and horses.

Theresa also found helpful the idea of taking her horse's hindquarters away. A horse that is unwilling to bend its head, or is so tense, locked up, braced up, and resistant that pulling his head around might just land the horse on top of you—that horse is so stiff, he's likely to fall. To overcome this stiffness, you take the horse's hindquarters away, remove its connection to the earth, so to speak, so that when you pull the reins around, you also urge him to move his hindquarters at the same time. That releases the brace and the resistance and reduces the danger to horse and rider. This attempt to get the horse to stop resisting is the equivalent of taking someone who is afraid and troubled into your arms and giving them a big hug. I've seen it work time and time again.

Another important lesson for Theresa was understanding the idea of changing eyes. A horse can see behind him, up to a point. There's a blind spot directly to the rear and out to about ten feet. If a horse doesn't really trust his rider or is bothered by him, he'll become very insecure every time the rider passes through that blind spot because Mother Nature tells the horse that he is vulnerable to whatever he can't see back there. However, a horse that is comfortable with his rider and trusts him completely will have no problem with the rider moving through his blind spot. So, the notion of getting a horse to change eyes—to be comfortable keeping you in view by turning his head slightly and watching you, first with one eye and then the other—is important. It is something that needs to be repeated thousands of times in order for the horse to become fully at ease. Theresa describes how this simple concept changed her relationship with her horses dramatically.

Finally, Theresa's story highlights the importance of getting a horse to hook on to you. Hooking begins by driving the horse around a circular corral. A round corral has no abrupt corners to force the horse to change stride or break his pace, which enables him to focus his attention on you. Because a round corral also enables you to direct the horse's energy into a smooth, continuous, flowing circle, you can then position yourself in the corral so that you literally draw the horse's energy toward you, first by moving in the same general direction that the horse is going, and then by slightly increasing your distance from him so that he feels compelled to move toward you. This is the essence of hooking on; a matter of getting a horse's undivided attention and being able to keep it. In Theresa's case, it was of utmost importance in building a better relationship with her Paint filly, a lesson that will serve her well both in the round corral and in life.

THERESA'S STORY

Like many others, I first came to Buck because I was at the end of my rope with my very troubled Thoroughbred mare. This mare was born on my farm on the vernal equinox nearly eleven years ago, and carried the evenness of that balanced day with her from birth. I didn't know then that her centeredness was so special. I only learned later, after she was betrayed by trainers who mistreated her as a three- and four-year-old, how essential that center is for a horse, and how elusive it is for a human.

Fortunately for Equinox and me, Buck came to Olympia, Washington, for a clinic the year my mare turned five. I was at my lowest point. Despite my investing a huge amount in training, she'd bucked me off several times that spring, and had become so touchy when saddling that she'd explode every time the cinch touched her chest. One day during saddling she pulled back hard and threw herself against the corral, tearing down a section of the three-board fence. This was a huge wreck. She ripped a twelve-inch gash in her side. My vet stitched her up; I put her out to pasture to heal and decided I wasn't going to let another trainer touch her again.

I knew I didn't know how to help her, but I didn't trust that anyone I'd seen so far could either. My mare was carefree before I'd started her education, and completely bottled up when she was returned to me, "finished." There had to be a better way.

I found that way when I watched Buck at the Olympia clinic. What he did in colt starting—with horses that could have given Equinox a run for the money in terms of troubles—was nothing short of miraculous. One horse was a three-year-old Appaloosa gelding that only a mother could love. This horse stalked into the round pen with ears pinned and neck braced, and turned to kick at Buck every chance it got. Buck's work with the Appy introduced me to the concept of yielding. Buck explained that this bold horse had been forcing its owner to yield ever since it was a foal. As a result of always being allowed to push everyone around, he'd developed into a juvenile delinquent, "socially bankrupt." So Buck taught the Appy what it should have learned since birth, how to yield to a leader. The horse left soft and forward.

I realized as I watched Buck that first time that I yielded to my horses as a habit; not just in the field when they crowded me for petting and I stepped aside, nor just in the barn aisle when I made room for that extra large draft horse shoulder as it moved by. I also yielded when I'd wake in the morning, think about riding, and say to myself that it was too windy, the field too slippery, the horse too green, and the potential trauma of riding too great. I yielded to Equinox every time I felt her fear. *Not* yielding was the first tough lesson I learned.

The second thing I took away from that weekend was understanding "changing eyes." My endurance horse that I rode regularly at the time had been really bad about standing in cross ties. He'd dance and twist his body around as far as he could to follow my movements. I'd never understood the concept of changing eyes, and I'm not proud of the fact I'd give him a good wallop to make him stand—not that it ever did any good. I hit him because I thought I needed to firm up with him, when all I needed was to get him used to me changing eyes. We worked on that after watching that first clinic, and things got a lot easier.

The third horse Buck worked with really caught my attention. This Paint was very sensitive, and as soon as Buck started to work it, it would just go still, its eye wary, and it would not want to move out with any life. I instantly recognized the look on that horse. This might have been my mare!

Somewhere along the line, I had tried to round-pen Equinox. I'd had one trainer help me with my Arabian, whose attention was hard to get and keep. She'd taught me how to hook the horse on in a round pen; I'd become pretty good at it, and it had helped us both. I figured this would be a good place to start with Equinox when she was about a year old. However, I saw her eye change the moment I sent her off. She was leaving me and I knew it, but I didn't understand why. It looked like resentment, and I pondered the matter a lot over the next week. I talked to all my horse friends; I'd spoiled her and she didn't want to work, was the favored theory.

After watching Buck that weekend, I knew to call Equinox's expression "shutting down," but that wasn't language I had heard before then. Back when I had the round-pen problem, I even thought for a while that Equinox, well-bred Thoroughbred that she was, was just too noble for me. You think such things when you don't understand what you're seeing.

Looking back, I think my instincts were right. Equinox was noble, but not because of her fancy bloodlines. Her nobleness is the nobility of her species, of subtlety and honesty. And I didn't know how to communicate with nobility. But Buck sure did. He explained while he worked the Paint mare that her type are some of the toughest horses for the uneducated to read because they look quiet, but they are really just shutting down. Buck put a lot of focus on this mare, changing things up all the time to keep her attention. He knew exactly how much pressure to apply and when to back off, before the horse got too worried. He introduced us to the concept of rewarding the smallest try as a way to build confidence in the mare. We watched the Paint come alive with try, doing anything Buck would ask of her.

Frankly, at that point in my education, most of what Buck did with the horse was too subtle for me to fully understand. But I saw the change, and I knew I needed to start paying a lot more attention to Equinox's smallest try.

Armed with this newfound knowledge after the clinic, I began to piece together the betrayals that had led to Equinox's troubles. And I had to admit, I couldn't just pin it on the trainer—I had to own up to the first few betrayals.

As Equinox grew, I'd introduced her to the gear of adulthood. She carried a bareback pad around the pasture. One day I decided to loop her lead rope around the fence post to adjust the pad. She stepped back, felt the first fear of confinement, and raced backwards, pulling the lead rope loose, and startling me. I'd never taught her to yield to pressure.

Another time after I'd hooked her in cross ties (even though I couldn't tie her), I went to pull off her splint boots. I'd built fear of confinement in her, so with the first swoosh of Velcro, she went rigid but nevertheless stood. Quickly, I bounced over to her other side (that changing-eye thing) and pulled the second boot off. The second Velcro sound was too much for her. She raced backwards, pulled one cross tie right out of the wall, and hung by the other that was now tangled in wheelbarrows and brooms. Somehow I managed to get Equinox untangled. I vowed then to get a trainer for her; I knew that I was well beyond my capabilities.

I don't want to speak badly of the trainers who worked with my mare. Both were gentle and effective with other horses, and they turned out a lot of nice riding mounts. And as I'm back in the saddle on my mare, I find quality there. Her lateral work is lovely, her stops as clean as you can get. She always takes the correct lead. But both trainers missed that shift in the eye; that first guarded moment when she was shutting down. When the trainers pushed her through, she learned how to go wherever horses go to escape the crudeness of humans.

The ultimate mistake—the one most costly to Equinox and the one that took me more than five years to solve—was the way the first trainer addressed her pulling-back issue. The trainer told me she had looped a rope around Equinox's girth, through the front legs and up through the halter, and then tied her to a solid eyebolt in a solid beam in the hay barn. Every time the mare pulled back, the rope around the girth would tighten. The theory was that as she moved forward, it would relieve the pressure, and she'd learn to not pull back. The trainer said she left her there alone in that barn for several hours at a time.

The problem with this old cowboy trick is that it just flat-out doesn't work. There was no release. More on point, the mare could not go forward. She was snubbed to a wall, so she braced backward, mentally and physically. I can write about this now without too much emotion, but this obsolete technique just about cost my mare her life.

After that first clinic as an observer, I'd practice the techniques Buck used on my other horses and then try them on Equinox. She was as braced as a board—there wasn't a spot on her body that wasn't tight. But we made progress. A big breakthrough came in the field one evening. More observant after being with Buck, I realized that she'd always step back when I'd put the halter on. I was just quick enough to get that halter on anyway. Nothing bold or violent—to me, but to Equinox, I might as well have roped her and hog-tied her. The resentment started right there, the moment I forced the halter on her.

I spent most of that evening just presenting the halter. If Equinox moved, I'd tell her no big deal, simply direct her to do something else other than go backwards, and then present the halter again. The first change was tiny: When I lifted the halter toward my waist, she waited. And then we quit. A week of those little moves led to big sighs and lots of lip licking and yawning, signs of a contented horse. By the end of the week Equinox would reach for that halter. That week in the field was the beginning of the turnaround in both of us.

But I still couldn't get the mare saddled, and I was scared to death to get back on her, so I decided to get her into one of Buck's colt-starting classes. Some friends recommended I ride one of my less troubled horses first in a horsemanship clinic so I'd have a better frame of reference. I signed up the next summer for my first horsemanship class in Ellensburg, Washington, where I gained a few more skills.

The following spring Equinox and I were enrolled in Buck's colt starting class in Lewiston, Idaho. I'd done every-thing I knew how to do to prepare her, but it was wholly in-adequate. Buck told me on the first day that I'd been doing what I thought was right, but that it wasn't going to cut it with this mare. I was devastated, but learned right then and there that humility is the beginning of real learning.

Buck found a brace in Equinox's shoulder and right front leg that was obvious to him, but I'd been blind to. As he worked her, Equinox looked like she was peg-legged. She planted that crutch leg and leaned on it with all of her one thousand pounds and told Buck that she needed that support. It was all she had left, and there was no way she was going to give it up to him.

Buck worked her from his horse and kept putting pressure on Equinox to reach out and back with that leg, to free the shoulder and free her mind. For a long time she had other ideas and gave the paying public a good show. She reared and struck out again and again, anything but give up that literal crutch, that solid, wooden leg that she could just lean into and hold onto when people betrayed her.

Buck warned us the mare might have to lay down, that she might not know she could move that leg. She didn't go down. Buck got through to her, and she realized she could shift her weight back, that she had three other legs and could lift and move that leg. She found freedom in movement. There really wasn't a dry eye in the house.

Buck built on that freedom and, when flagging the colts, paid some special attention to Equinox. She flew around that arena, lapping the other colts, exhibiting every bit of her Thoroughbred breeding, but it didn't bring a horse race-spectator crowd response from those of us watching. We knew we were watching her work out a lot of stuff that should have never been put in her to begin with. She had to run because she'd been so bunched up for so long, she just had to get it out. While he moved the others down the arena as a herd, Buck let her on by for another, then another, then a third lap. He let her learn to move until he finally began crowding her just a bit to see if she'd turn to join the other horses at the end of the arena. If not, he'd just back off, give Equinox an opening, and let her on by, until finally, she could travel through a smaller opening, free and full and then, settled, she moved down the arena with the other horses. I rode her at that clinic. We walked, trotted, and loped. And we went home grinning from ear to ear.

I ended that year with Equinox in another of Buck's horsemanship classes that fall. Twice, my mare set off bucking, and twice, the lessons of colt starting helped me stay on. The moment she started bucking, I took her hindquarters away— even though she was pretty athletic and able to toss me around. The second she paused, I pushed her in forward gear and just rode on out of it as if we did this every day. Free forward motion was the key to everything with this mare.

It was at this clinic I realized we had to do a lot more exposure on the ground to changing eyes. Both times she set off bucking, another horse had bolted into her left eye. The second time I was not as prepared, and almost came off. But, as Buck has told us numerous times, staying on doesn't have as much to do with riding skill as it does with resolve. And when it comes to staying on a horse, I have a lot of resolve. I was headed over her shoulder like a lawn dart when I grabbed the saddle horn, wrenched myself back up, grabbed the right rein, pulled her head around, kicked the hindquarters free, and again legged her on forward. Not bad, I thought as we trotted on down the arena, my friends cheering "Go, girl!"

However, even by the last day of the clinic, Equinox never completely settled. She was just too worried to handle the exposure, and I didn't have enough to offer this mare. She was just too far ahead. I decided to ride my other horses and to catch up.

The good news is, I was on the right track with Buck. Plus, I had a community of friends further along in Buck's approach than I am, who were willing to help, particularly Mike and Deanie Hosker of Ellensburg (they sponsor Buck's clinic each year, and they start colts and teach). Charlie Anderson from Olympia has a superb riding school that promotes these techniques, and there was also Cheryl Smith, her neighbor and teaching partner. All of these folks have become dear friends over the years, and have encouraged me to keep at it.

I ended up taking two years off with Equinox. It seemed the more I learned, the more I realized how little I knew. The next year at Buck's clinic I rode Skeeter, a happy-go-lucky Arabian that my husband rode maybe six times a year. I figured Skeeter would be a good project; I rode him with great joy that year, and we helped each other.

My next horse on my journey to catch up with Equinox was a Quarter Horse mare I found standing up to her hocks in clay in a paddock in Wenatchee, Washington. My husband had business there one weekend, and since one of my lifelong friends, Lea Headley, lived there, I went along. She also happens to be a really handy horsewoman, so we made arrangements to ride together. As we rode out around town, she told me the horse her daughter Rachel had raised, rodeoed, and taken to college was now just standing around. Her daughter, Rachel Kellogg, was a Hot Shot firefighter with the United States Forest Service, and with traveling all over the country, she couldn't keep the mare. Would I like to see her? I said yes, though I told Lea that with other horses at home, I had no intention of getting another. But the mare was beautiful and had a kind, sensitive eye. Before the day was over, I was on my way to owning a new horse.

When I hauled over a few weeks later to ride with Rachel, the mare was cleaned up and standing on the gravel drive. She was huge—more than sixteen hands, twelve hundred pounds, and all muscle. I'd never bothered to ask her name before.

"Tornado," Rachel said proudly.

"Tornado?"

Rachel laughed. "Yeah, because I like to wind her up and off we go!"

This girl is a former junior rodeo champion, fights the worst forest fires in America for a living, and named her horse Tornado. I realized I might be in trouble. "I'm going to call her Blossom," I told Rachel right then and there. (I later named her *Regala*, "gift" in Spanish, because she truly has been a great partner on my way to becoming a horsewoman.)

Rachel wanted to show me what my new little Tornado/Blossom could do, so we took her over to a local arena. Rachel hopped on and, sure enough, she wound her up and off they flew. They looked like a Tasmanian Devil. First, they galloped one circle, winding it down to less than ten meters, and back out to a full circle, straight into a flying lead change and back down into another tight circle. On out and down the arena, one roll back, then another, another flying lead change across the arena, and back down to us in a sliding stop.

Rachel handed over the reins, and I threw a leg over Tornado. The second my seat hit the saddle, the mare jetted off. I did the only thing any self-respecting Buck student would do and took her hindquarters away, although I realized quickly that she had no bend whatsoever and I'd have to be careful not to flip her. After about a dozen times taking the hindquarters away and lots of bringing her head around and stroking her, I finally got Tornado to the point where, when I'd release her, she'd walk out without racing away, and I figured I'd live.

Well, it just about killed Rachel to watch me gentle her Tornado. She figured I was ruining her well-oiled flying machine. She asked if she could ride her one more time to really show me what she could do. Sure, I said, and climbed up on the rail to watch the dust devils fly.

"There!" she said, handing Tornado back over to me, with the implication that this is how you ride this mare and don't forget it.

What I brought home was a very talented mare with two speeds: walk and gallop. Regala (I had changed her name) was also braced in about every corner of her body. Rachel was a hell of a rider, and Regala was an athlete, so the two had stayed upright.

I rode this mare with Buck in two clinics that summer and fall. We did a lot of flexing and bending, and I got a nice trot on her. However, when it came to loping, I hung onto her mouth the whole time, as she pulled me out of the saddle with each huge stride.

As any of us who ride with Buck for a while will learn, he doesn't pick at you. He just puts his learning out there and lets you find it as you need it. If someone is getting in trouble, he'll intervene to keep him or her safe, but mostly Buck takes the same approach with us as he takes with the horse. He sets up the situation and then lets us keep searching until we find the answer. Sometimes it takes one day. Sometimes it takes years.

After watching me fly around on this mare for two clinics, Buck decided it was time to intervene. On the second day of the second clinic, he'd instructed the group to lope out on a loose rein. I put my mare into her only loping speed—a dead gallop—and let the reins go slack. Buck let us go twice around the arena, Regala picking up speed the whole time.

When we went flying by at a dead run, Buck realized I was not going to use an ounce of common sense and slow her down on my own, so he boomed, "Theresa, take a hold of that mare!" When I grabbed up the reins and pulled to no avail, he refined his instruction; "Take a hold until you get to the feet . . . then release."

This was an epiphany. I'd been trying to rein Regala in, and I'd even slowed her a bit, but I'd never been firm enough to get to her feet and cause her to break stride. It is hard to describe how important that lesson was to me. (It even carried over into other areas of my life. I've worked most of my career in executive management positions; knowing when to take hold is an essential skill in business, and one that I really sharpened up after Buck's timely instruction.)

I can still feel the moment when Regala finally broke stride. I immediately released and we got two strides at a lope before her speed picked up. So again, I took hold, got the change in the feet, released, and felt the success of a few more normal loping strides. Over time, we achieved more and more easy strides on a loose rein.

With Buck, it is all about knowing when it is time to be soft and subtle and when to take hold and mean it, to apply as much pressure as it takes to get a change—and that was a lot with this mare. Not to generalize about gender, but like most of my girlfriends, I struggle with really getting assertive with a horse, just as many guys must work to be gentle. To be a true horseman requires both.

The horse is such a powerful teacher because it has a much broader range of expression than the human. We tend to find a rather narrow range of behavior that we're comfortable with and operate within it. But the horse runs the spectrum; when their behavior is too fine for us, we miss what they need, and when they are too bold for us, we miss what they need. Being able to match them all along the way is what Buck is trying to teach us. Regala gave me what I needed to know: that it was okay to take hold of Equinox and shut her down when her expressions ranged to the big, bold end of the spectrum.

Finally, last spring, after a year on Skeeter and a year on Regala, I felt I was ready to go back to Equinox with some new tools.

The saddling problem had continued to perplex me during the two-year break from riding her. A number of good friends helped me. We'd used every technique we could find: letting her grow accustomed to a rope around her middle, and getting her front end loosened up so she would not brace that front right leg. I'd even roped her hind legs, which is an exercise in Buck's groundwork book that most people skip on over because it can feel pretty scary.

A horse is smarter than a human, and Equinox knew that none of those techniques was a saddle. It was the tightening of the cinch she really feared, as I discovered one Saturday in February 2003 when I learned how to never send her off center again during saddling. This discovery wasn't my own; it was a matter of putting together what Buck taught about putting pressure on and knowing when to release. It was also enhanced by work I'd done with Mike and Deanie, who taught that flagging horses is putting on enough pressure to put them out of their comfort zone, but not so much as to frighten them beyond the point where they can handle it— the same technique Buck had applied in that first clinic with the sensitive Paint mare.

In practical terms, flagging means reaching in with the flag, touching the horse, and quickly retreating, so just about the time the horse thinks the fluttering thing will kill him, it goes away and he realizes he is still fine. But then, here it comes again, and it is still horribly frightening, but it's not a fright that lasts. It is a small fright, like a bird flying up into their line of sight in the field: worth a start, but not a bolt. Using this technique, I had worked Regala into a comfortable place with the flag within an hour, so later I could ride her with it flapping around any old way, and she didn't care.

It occurred to me that Equinox had finally learned to tolerate the saddle more out of a desire to do right than a true acceptance of it; the fear was always still lurking. So, I took the advance-and-retreat method and the saddle into the round pen with me and put it to the test. I started easy; goosing her a little in the cinch area with my hands and backing out so quickly she only had time to flinch and move a step or two. I worked slowly, from quick touch to longer, deeper pressure all around the girth area, but always releasing if she showed the beginnings of fear. Soon, she was standing, slack-jawed and with hip cocked, while I applied pressure all over the normally touchy area.

I figured it was time for the saddle. Equinox braced the minute I brought it up off the ground. I threw it on the way I'd been taught by Buck, so it swung high and wide and settled smooth and centered on her back. Before it even had time to settle and the mare's feet had time to get moving, I pulled it off.

Equinox looked at me in complete relief. I rubbed her and we did it again; just a quick brushing of the saddle on her back and then it was off again, and while her foot still had to move a step, she stayed. I moved her back in position and swung again, letting the saddle settle a second as her eye looked back and her shoulder started to tighten, and then off it came. We went on like this for another half dozen times until I left the saddle on and she accepted it on her back. I let her stand there and contemplate the rightness of her situation.

But rather than advancing to the next step—working with the girth—I surprised the mare and pulled the saddle off again. She rewarded my patience by dropping her head nearly to the ground while her eyes rolled back. Then she yawned and her tongue rolled out and around, all signs of a relaxed horse. I let her finish enjoying the success of the moment, then picked up and swung the saddle again, this time letting it fall in place and moving around to the other side as if I would drop the cinch.

Equinox's right eye looked warily at me. I fiddled a bit before moving back around and pulling off the saddle. She stood quietly while I contemplated how sore my shoulders were getting, and then I swung the saddle up again. This time I moved around, dropped the cinch, bounced it around a bit, went back, and pulled the saddle off. Swinging it over the next time, I swiftly reached under her to take hold of the cinch. When I saw her front right leg brace, I backed out and pulled the saddle off. Equinox was starting to get it. She understood that she was setting the pace. She relaxed.

I swung again; reached under, saw no brace, so touched her chest with the cinch, which garnered a slight flick of the tail, and so off the whole saddle came again. Then back again, pulling the cinch up to actually put pressure on her this time, which I then quickly released. But this time, I left the saddle on. She said this was okay, so we did this a half dozen times; up until it touched her, back down loose again; touch; release; touch with more pressure, release; touch; release; until I was sure I could go ahead and loop the latigo through and move on.

But I didn't move on. I took the saddle off and let her ponder this new state of affairs, which she did with a frank look back at me; a cocking of the hip and a dropping of the head. Up the saddle went again, the girth brought up snug, the latigo pulled down—and then released. We repeated the whole girth process with the latigo; pulling down tight; re-leasing; tight; release; until she was fine with that, and I un-saddled her. We sat enjoying the slow, easy day, and I saddled her again.

This time I said, Okay, kiddo, you're ready for this latigo to go through the girth and past that point of no return, which is when the cinch is partly pulled up but not yet secured, so if Equinox were to blow—which she had done as regularly as Old Faithful—we could have a wreck on our hands.

I took it easy, slowly snugging it up, ready to pull tight fast if forced to, but Equinox was just fine with the whole thing. So, saddle secured, we walked off. And there it was: the braced right front leg, short striding for at least one time around the round pen, but Equinox walked it out.

I unsaddled the mare, then saddled her right up again, this time just moving right along. I watched for tension, and finding none, I walked her off, with less brace this time, and which worked out more quickly. I unsaddled and saddled her again, and this time when she walked off with no brace, I asked for an easy trot. The cinch grabbed her a bit and she quickened her pace, but she settled back pretty quickly, so we just got right to work doing groundwork we'd not done in a year.

Novices watching would have thought me nuts. From their seat outside the ring of knowledge, they would not have seen her move. After all, although Equinox's feet stayed almost stock-still during each saddling, she was telling me each and every time just how much she could tolerate. I'd read all those signs before, but I used to think, "I just have to get her through this." So I'd snap the rope to stop her feet and just get her saddled and watch as, braced and resentful, she'd work it off, sometimes bucking, sometimes just walking off, but never truly accepting. I was only fooling myself. Equinox so resented me by the time the saddling was done that no matter how forgiving her nature, she just flat-out couldn't trust me on her back. Frightened, she had to take over and try and get me off. If I couldn't be trusted with this thing that was obviously so important to her, how could I be trusted with anything else?

Finally, last spring, after four long years of work and worry, I rode my mare with confidence. Mike and Deanie hosted a clinic at Charlie's, so I knew I'd get a lot of support with her. It was wonderful. When she got lost, I helped her find her way. When she got nervous, I settled her. When she spooked and jumped, I rode through it like I'd ride any other horse through a little worry. In other words, after four years of treating her like she was damaged goods, I treated her like a horse. Any horse. A horse without history. A horse that just needs a little direction and support and help along the way.

Could I have had those rides a year before? No. But at some point, I had to get there, and with the help of Buck and all the skilled horsemen he's developed in our community in

Washington, I caught up to my mare. Not all at once, but a little bit, over time. Could a more skilled horseman have done it sooner? Of course; but he or she would have turned the mare back over to me, and I would not have been able to support her.

And I'm still learning. Even with the success on Equinox last spring, I still was not ready to ride her with Buck last summer. When you ride with Buck, you really come into your own pressure, and it's not something to take lightly. So, I rode Regala at the clinics, and Equinox at home.

But I saw something at a clinic in Tacoma that made an impression. A tentative young rider with an Arab struggled to keep her horse's attention. During the groundwork, it ran all over her. When under saddle, it looked like someone had stuck the throttle on high and the steering wheel locked in a sharp right turn. The horse would jet off, the rider would try to take its hindquarters away, and it would just run circles in place. This horse looked like the Calvin character in *Calvin and Hobbes* after an entire morning of eating frosted sugar bombs cereal—he had a serious case of attention deficit disorder.

Buck let the pair struggle a day or so. The girl was getting a little more coordination in her efforts, but she was still like a gnat on an elephant. When Buck stepped in and took the lead rope, we learned what presence could do. He locked this horse's mind on his and held it within seconds. He did a lead-by or two to show the Arab he knew where its feet were and that he was in control of them. But he did not get physical at all with this horse—he simply commanded respect with his presence. After about thirty seconds with Buck on the other end of the lead rope, if the horse could have saluted, he would have.

To demonstrate his mental hold, Buck handed the horse back to the owner and walked away, working the entire way around the arena, the horse following his every move as he wove in and out among other horses. When Buck had asked the horse to stay put, it stayed. Even after Buck handed the horse back to the rider, feet stilled and mind settled, the horse's eye followed Buck's every move for a full ten minutes. Finally, when it was obvious to the horse that Buck wasn't coming back for him, he started jigging and pushing his owner around again. It was one of the most astounding things I'd seen Buck do. And I became convinced that truly taking hold is as much about presence as it is technique.

I realized that this was the missing element for me and Equinox: presence. I'd worked through a hundred things with her, but there was one thing I hadn't done: saddle and ride her unsupported by other horses, friends, or clinicians.

So one winter Saturday, I rose early, carefully put on my best cowgirl gear, cleaned my tack, gathered Equinox up from the field, groomed her until she shone, and then took her into the arena and saddled her. No other horses were around for support. No friends. No clinicians. Just me and my mare. The saddling was fine—that demon had been slain. I did all the rituals Buck taught us in colt starting, which I call the preflight safety check: checking all four feet to make sure everything is operating properly; unhooking the hind end in both directions and bringing the front across both sides; leading and backing; bridling—that is, checking to see if any additional groundwork is necessary before the rider mounts.

Equinox was pretty good through it all, so I bumped her up to the rail and threw a leg over. That first ride wasn't anything to brag about; we just got through it together. But we did it. The rides have greatly improved this spring and summer, with an occasional setback. Buck had told me after that first colt-starting clinic with Equinox that she and I would get around her trouble, and I hung on those words. I'm pleased to say, we've done it.

Buck gives a moving lecture at some clinics where he describes the steps involved in the making of a bridle horse. He demonstrates and describes the various tack used along the way. I like this demonstration because it symbolizes the journey the horseman is on. My favorite part is when he explains the *bosalita*, a pencil-thin bosal with a leather tie that is secured in the forelock. Buck explains that the bosalita has no real function; it is jewelry to honor the horse and his accomplishments.

Last year after he gave this demonstration for us and explained the bosalita, I came home and wrote this poem:

I yearn to earn the right to wear the bosalita someday.
As I'm passing through the Light at the end of my life,
I hope I'll feel my Lord carefully tie it in my hair,
A symbol that I allowed the Master to complete His work
     with me.
That after I balked and braced, I yielded to His hands,

When I stalled out, uncertain, I learned to move forward,
*   freely following His lead,*
That when I flew in fear, not caring for my fate, but only for
*   my fear,*
I learned to slow my feet and wait on Him, until sure of Him,
I ran with faith, swift and certain and true, in the paths He
*   made for me.*

CHAPTER 3

OVERCOMING THE PAST

I was very interested in Laurie's story, as her childhood was unhappy and unfulfilling, much like my own. Laurie didn't have much of a family growing up. Her dad was an aggressive alcoholic, just like mine. Although my brother and I had to stick around and endure our father's rage, Laurie was shuttled from one uncaring caretaker to another. Both situations create children who never feel wanted or loved. This kind of up-bringing is hard to overcome, but Laurie has given her all to letting go of her past hurts, and tries to look ahead to a more positive future.

Meeting Laurie and hearing her story reminded me of the notion of enduring hardship. There are a lot of people who don't have the luxury of a basic, normal life. They may have tragedy to deal with—hardships, things that happen to them that just don't seem fair. (Each of you, please make a note to self: *Life isn't fair.*) There are so many bad things that happen to so many good people; as much as you try to make sense of it, the bottom line is, countless random things can happen to a person—the important thing is how we deal with them.

In my first book, *The Faraway Horses,* I revealed some of the most private, personal things that have made me who I am today. I did it to share my own experience with others who may have had just as difficult a road to travel as I did when I was young. What I've learned and hope to share with all of you is that rotten beginnings don't always mean rotten endings. Sometimes good comes from trouble and hardship, and I tell you honestly, I'm a sap for that stuff. I love watching Disney movies with my daughter because I'm really into happy endings. Hopefully, I'll never get too old or jaded or cynical to where Old Yeller's death means nothing to me.

I also shared my personal story because I wanted to show people that in order to move forward with our lives, we have to let go of the things from the past that hold us back. Those old hurts and bad feelings will drag you down every time; leaving them in the past where they belong is the only way you're going to have a different future. Sometimes you're not going to get closure; things won't always be tied up with a nice, neat little ribbon. A lot of people expect that happy ending, and they're sure to be disappointed when it doesn't happen, so they get to thinking that their entire life is a failure because of this one thing in their past that still bothers them. The thing is, as much as we'd like it to, life hardly ever turns into "happily ever after" on its own—sometimes you just have to let it go, move on, and make a new future for yourself.

When folks are trying to work through hardships in their lives, the accepted approach is often that everyone needs to give them encouragement and positive reinforcement to help this healing process along. For example, both Laurie and my brother and I had the hardship of an abusive, alcoholic father, a hell of a thing for a kid to have to deal with. And there's no question about it—having others around you who support you and encourage you is a real blessing. Unfortunately, not everyone has that kind of support system. Some folks, like Laurie and my brother and I, had only ourselves to lean on. When you have no one to turn to, the grim reality is that you have to pull yourself up by your own bootstraps. You're not always going to have the support group that you would like, but that does not make it okay to wallow in failure or mediocrity, or to allow needless burdens from the past to bring you down.

I think of life as a big cake. The support and love of the people around us—whose positive reinforcement helps that healing happen—is the icing on the cake. Now, I'm perfectly content eating cake that doesn't have any frosting on it at all— it's okay with me. As for you, there's always the chance that you won't get icing on your piece of cake. Then you have options; you can either eat it as it is and call it good, or toss it away because it has no icing. Somewhere along the line, the human spirit has an opportunity to make a change of direction, wherever it happens to be headed.

A lot of people find it remarkable that I've been able to put my past to rest, in spite of all the troubles I encountered as a youngster. Well, I don't live in the past, but I do look back sometimes to find important lessons in the good and bad things that happened. I'm careful how I live my life today. You see, there are a lot of people that accept the notion that if you grew up in a home where a parent was abusive, you are pretty much going to end up the same way. If your father was an alcoholic, it's pretty much a sure thing you're going to be one, too. I don't believe that, and I've met too many people in my life that have prevailed over what some psychologist assured them was their fate. We all have free choice, and opportunities to do things with our lives. We just don't always take them.

Some things that happened when I was a kid are kind of embarrassing to share, but here's one. Every now and then, as I'm getting ready to go to a clinic and work with people and their horses, I'll be cleaning up in the morning, getting ready for the day, and I'll glance in the bathroom mirror and get a look at the roll of toilet paper hanging innocently next to the toilet. To most folks, toilet paper doesn't have any big, significant meaning in their lives, but it does for me. It's one of those things that get etched in your mind, and can take you back in the blink of an eye.

One particular evening, my brother Smokie and I had tried our best to go to bed early because that was the best way to avoid our father's drunken outrage. If we could get to bed early before Dad became really intoxicated, it might not even occur to him that we two boys were in the house, and he might just sit and get drunk in the dark by himself. Unhappily, his pickled brain often did send him thoughts of us, and he'd get us up and holler and scream at us all night long for anything and everything. I remember sitting, night after night, at an oak table that he had made himself. (For such a tough guy, he was pretty handy; not a terribly kind person, but a capable one.) To this day, I could probably replicate every grain of that oak table for you, because we learned to keep our eyes down, to never look up. If you happened to glance up when he was already on a drunken diatribe, he interpreted looking at him as a provocation that was guaranteed to get you knocked across the room. So we always looked down at that table.

On this one night we'd gone to bed early, but Dad came into our bedroom and yanked us out of our bunk beds anyway, then made us go into the kitchen. Now, Dad was kind of a tightwad. He'd always turn the heat way down at night, not much caring if we were warm or not. So we sat there in what felt like Antarctica.

Dad had somehow decided, through his drunken stupor, that my brother and I must have been using too much toilet paper, because he believed the roll was getting smaller way faster than in the past. This was the topic of our intellectual exchange for the evening. We spent the next four or five hours listening, crying, getting beat on, knocked across the room, picked up and thrown back into our chairs. And all through this endless horror, the thing that kept filling my head about the whole deal was that this issue of toilet paper consumption was going to boil up to the surface again probably a dozen times over the next four or five days before he finally let it go. He had a hard time changing gears, letting go, and just moving on.

When I'm on the road and I have a chance to talk to folks, I work with them to let go of something that has already happened, something that embarrasses them. I try to help them recognize and remove some personal issue they may have with their horse, husband, or child. I make a point to talk to them about moving on, being able to change gears and not feel like everything has to be resolved, or that everything has to have closure. Like I said, you're not always going to get closure, and you don't necessarily need it, but you *do* need to move on. At least, that's something I've found to be true in my life. I'm not a tortured soul because of what I went through as a kid, but I'm definitely the wiser for it, and I hope I'm able to share the wisdom I gained from those early days with others I meet on the trail. I may not be an intellectual compared to some folks, but I survived some pretty tough life experiences growing up; I share them so that people know they're not alone. Not anymore.

And that's really what it's all about for me, how we deal with whatever comes along, and how we can help others get through—and beyond their own problems. Living in the past can become a habit, and humans aren't the only ones who do this; It can also become a habit with horses. So as I comment on people's stories throughout this book, I hope you'll notice the common thread—what works with horses often works with people, as well.

I'm gratified to know that even with a learning disability, Laurie's daughter understood the life lessons I try to incorporate into my clinics. And once Laurie realized that her subtle, fearful behaviors were causing her horse to react poorly, she understood that *she* had created an endless loop of negativity between the two of them, and only she could put an end to it. She learned that interacting properly with a horse is like learning how to dance. She had to learn to lead with confidence, and her horse had to learn to follow her lead with confidence. Once the two of them got that straightened out, they began acting as a real team, moving as one, neither partner more important than the other, both dependent on the other to do their job and fulfill their responsibilities with confidence and grace. That moment of complete mutual respect and trust marks the beginning of a relationship between a horse and human that's one of the most special relationships you can have with an animal.

LAURIE'S STORY

The first time I saw Buck Brannaman, at one his clinics in 1998, I was struck by his ability to communicate with horses. Buck would get in the arena with a troubled horse, and in no time the horse would focus on Buck, responding to every silent, subtle movement of Buck's head or body. I was also very impressed with Buck's talent for imparting his profound personal wisdom to everyone in the audience, almost without their being aware that a life lesson was being presented. Even my daughter, who has a learning disability, understood him and his messages very well.

When I was growing up, I spent time in different homes. My parents were having a lot of trouble, so I stayed in about five different homes—a place in New Jersey, a farm in Central New Hampshire, and so on. As far as I know, I was saved from a lot of problems by being sent away, because I didn't see a lot of the alcoholism that went on with my dad, which eventually led to my parents' divorce. Of course, nobody talked about it. Nobody mentioned what the real problems were. We all just dealt with it, and went on with life.

Years later when I was lucky enough to attend one of Buck Brannaman's clinics, I learned that Buck's early life was very hard, too, but it inspired me to see that he never dwelt on it or let it hold him back. It's part of his life, part of his story, but he's gone on. The way he's turned his life into something so healthy and positive made me realize that that's what I needed to do as well. Buck showed me that if you live your life filled with negatives, you'll end up with a kid, or a marriage—or even a horse—with a lot of negatives too. It's not easy and it's sometimes scary, but if you're going to get anywhere and be happy in your life, you have to find some way to get past the negatives. Your life depends on it!

One of the first things I told Buck about my horse was, "This horse is really pushy. What's going on?" He looked at me and said, "Well, who do you think is pushing who?" I laughed at first, but then his real message hit me. All of my defense mechanisms were affecting how the horse reacted to me. I'd been scared of life, scared of so much, and Buck got me to realize that I was scaring the horse and causing it to react negatively to me. *I* was the problem, not the horse!

Buck made it clear that my own fear was creating all the problems between my horse and me. My dread and tension was impossible for my horse to ignore, eventually affecting him just as negatively as it was affecting me. For my horse's sake and for the sake of the relationship we shared, I had to let go of that tension and stress. I didn't have to accept and hold onto my past hurts and fears—I had the choice to let go of them and move past them. Buck's gentle guidance helped me make the right choice.

Buck's wisdom is very basic: It's all about how you learn to run your life, how you learn to run your horse's life. Buck showed me how fear can undermine everything you do, how foolish it is to be impatient, and how cruel it is to withhold affection and respect. He was talking about horses, but I was hearing advice about life. I understood perfectly, because I had been starved in a lot of ways, emotionally and physically; people didn't even care about whether I was fed or not. My life was empty, and it hurt. Buck helped me to see that my life wasn't really empty at all. I had a lot to be thankful for.

Another thing Buck taught me is that to communicate, you not only have to make yourself heard clearly, but you also have to really listen to others. I have a habit of barging through things—work, play, life in general—probably out of the fear and insecurity that overrides everything else. I forget to be patient, I forget to listen, I forget that things are going to be okay. Buck's taught me how to slow down and listen, to others and to my own heart, by showing me how to listen to what my horse is telling me.

I learned how not to communicate from my family and from the life I had away from my home. My father was never easy to talk to. Nothing we kids did was good enough for him, and nothing we said interested him. I learned pretty quickly how to put up a strong wall and hide behind it. But Buck managed to break that ingrained habit of mine. He leads folks from one thing to the next, builds on small things to bigger things, shows you that you'll get nowhere if you and your horse can't communicate, just as you'll get nowhere in life if you can't communicate well with people.

What works in disciplining a horse also works in self-discipline. It's a never-ending loop: as you look at what your horse's problem is, it causes you look at what your own problems are, and you go right on through and you fix them, then leave them behind and go on to the next thing. For example, my personal fear created negative tension in my horse, which in turn made me even more nervous and tense. Once I realized that my horse's problem actually began with me, I was able to turn things around for both of us. Just like Buck said, when you really look and listen to your horse, he'll tell you what's wrong. Once you figure out the problem, everything starts to connect together and fall into place. One lesson builds on another, and the more you understand what you're doing with your animal, the more you understand about yourself.

It's like you're pushing yourself to the limits of what you want from yourself through the horse, and vice versa. What you expect from him is what you expect from yourself. In learning this lesson, you also learn to require respect from the animal as well as from yourself. The loop begins by communicating with the horse through discipline, figuring out what direction you want to go, and then following that path. This reflects back on you; what you want to accomplish, how you're going to get there, your direction and your path. The circle of learning repeats itself again and again.

I've always been drawn to horses, but I never realized what kind of rapport I could have with these animals. Part of my fascination with that special rapport is a reflection of the work I'm doing on my communication skills. Every day I try to get better at it.

When I first met Buck, I had no real appreciation of what it meant to ride well, or what real horsemanship was. I guess I used to think it was about how fast you could go, how high you could jump, how many ribbons you won. Buck has shown me that those things mean nothing. It's more important to have purpose and a goal. To achieve any goal, you have to look forward and leave the past and all its troubles behind you. I'm still living on the farm where my father lived and died, and I still see the discord among other members of my family, so turning my back on the past is difficult. Some of the same things that affected my father are affecting other members of the family, and I see it every day. It's really hard, but I keep trying.

One thing that helps me put the past behind me is to focus on what's happening right now. Buck is very adamant that you must be completely real and completely honest with yourself and your animal right now, right in this very moment. What happened thirty seconds ago means nothing to the horse; it's what you're doing right this second that he will respond to. I work hard to keep that in mind—to live authentically in the moment.

Even though Buck's own personal road has been long and hard, to see how he's overcome it all is a real inspiration. You see him and you say, "Hey, if he can get past all that, I'm sure I can overcome whatever problems I've had, too. I can certainly get on with things and create that positive circle for myself." Life is a path, a journey, and it's also a never-ending circle. The more you challenge yourself, the more things come easily, and the better you get at whatever it is you've set your mind to do.

Buck has helped me realize that a lot of a horseman's success or failure has to do with his own attitude. The key is to avoid creating a bad habit to begin with, and to focus on what's ahead of you. My life has been one of real contrasts, some great highs and some terrible lows. I'm probably the only member of my family who has managed to step away from the negative pull of our past—not only because of the incredible people who believe in me, but also because of the incredible people I've met and learned from along the way, like Buck Brannaman.

CHAPTER 4

WORKING THINGS THROUGH

Have you ever been with a couple—whether they're married or just dating, it makes no difference—that didn't appear to have much of a relationship? A couple where one or the other, or maybe both at the same time, will nag to the point where the other completely shuts down? Maybe they don't talk at all, or just sort of act like they're not there with their partner— they're not together, in the mental and emotional sense. When you see that, you realize that they've been acting this way for so long, they don't even know what they're doing anymore. If they could watch themselves, they'd be ashamed and embar- rassed. But living like this can become a habit. What I've found interesting is that when someone is nagging you—trying to impose his or her will in a way that is so relentless, there is never an opportunity for you to accept or reject it—you begin to feel trapped. The pressure is always on, and the options that you might otherwise have offered are not only not even recognized to be right or wrong, they're not even acknowledged in any way. That relentless sort of attack can be a way of life for some people.

Folks will come to my clinics to have me work with their children, and I actually have to say to some of them, "Look, you're not allowed to talk to this child for the next three hours. They need to work this out, so please—nothing from the audience." And I might even tell the child, "You don't need to pay any attention to your parents or anyone else outside of this arena as long as you're here studying with me." I try as hard as I can to present an example for the parents who are relentlessly oppressing this kid so that perhaps they will better understand how to get something accomplished with their child. Hopefully, the parent will observe their child making positive steps, and will try to discover what took place, and how it happened. Often I'll get some things accomplished with kids that they'll find remarkable, and the whole thing boils down to "release." Remember that word, *release*, remember *letting go*.

When you are trying to solve a problem, you're in a dilemma. You'll feel a certain amount of pressure, and maybe even a certain amount of stress. As you work through the problem and finally begin to solve it, there is a release of that pressure and stress. As a teacher, I look for the moment when a student's solution to the problem starts to take shape, and then I leave them alone with it. I want them to really feel and enjoy the release; that moment of peace and tranquility that comes from having solved a tough problem. It's important not to take that moment away from anyone, and I try hard to fix things up in a way that allows my ideas to become their ideas, without them realizing it. And when it happens, I want folks to understand that they shouldn't be robbed of that glory of discovery. Instead, we should revel in the success of others and help them build their confidence and pride in a job well done. You shouldn't ever take credit for someone else making a good decision—that should always belong to them, even if you did everything you could to set up the situation so they would come upon the idea themselves.

Letting go is really a matter of encouraging a horse, or another person, to let go of whatever it is they think they need to protect themselves. Letting go of defenses is the only way a horse or rider will accomplish anything positive. It's not a matter of submission; it's more about giving—giving willingly without feeling that you're being forced into it.

I also encourage my students to strive for lightness. Everyone wants to be able to get something done with very little fuss, and having a light hand helps accomplish that. Lightness can be a thousand different things, but it's always positive. One way to achieve that inner lightness is to approach a problem with the idea of doing just a bit less than what you think it might actually take to get the job done. Now you can't do this while driving a nail or digging a posthole or dealing with something that isn't alive and feeling and thinking, but animals have insights and emotions. They can make good and bad decisions; they may be afraid, grow confident, or become upset.

I recommend that my students begin by offering the horse a bit less strong direction, to sort of sneak up on what it takes to get the job done and, in the process, discover what might annoy or bother the horse. You do only what it takes to be effective—not try to hammer a nail with a sledgehammer.

So I advise folks to approach situations with an assertive nature—confident and assertive, but absolutely not aggressive—letting it be known that what you want to happen is not open for discussion. You do just what it takes to get the job done, but no more. This is the time to release, to back off, and allow the idea to take shape in the other person's, or the horse's, mind. It's the most important lesson in the art of conversation, no matter who you're trying to communicate with. It's all about learning to keep your mouth shut, learning to listen and watch, learning how to release and let go.

So many times when it comes to working with kids, people underestimate their abilities. Often, Forrest, my foster dad, would send me out at just about daylight to wrangle the geldings. That meant gathering the older geldings out of a pasture that was about three miles long and about one mile wide. To top it off, the land wasn't flat, and it was filled with cedars, cottonwoods, aspens, sagebrush, and countless hills and gullies, a multitude of places where the horses could hide. Most of the horses were generally uncooperative, especially if you didn't understand where you needed to be to get the job done.

I loved Forrest so much. To my mind, he was my true father, and I so wanted him to be proud of me and approve of me; I wanted him to know that there wasn't a job he wanted done that I wouldn't rush out to accomplish, to show him that I was strong and smart and successful. Well, he sent me out there and told me to bring in all the horses, so that's what I was going to do.

When I finally got back to the barn, I was pretty happy. I had a bunch of horses in the corral. The saddle horse that I was on was bone-tired; he had worked hard and was covered with sweat from one end to the other. I was exhausted, too. Both of us had really worked to get these horses in. And I guess I just got in such a hurry trying to stay caught up with the herd that I didn't think to count them.

It turned out I had missed three. Those three were not going to be used that day, but my foster dad said, "Son, when you wrangle those geldings, you have to wrangle them all." With that, he sent me back out on a horse that was almost too tired to even move, so we had to go at a very slow pace and it took us hours. I finally found the other three geldings and brought them in, but I was still fuming about it, and at first refused to talk about it. I was feeling sorry for myself, and I wanted him to let me off the hook. I thought he was being unreasonable and much too hard on me, and I was very upset with him.

I didn't realize that Forrest was allowing me to work at this problem. He was allowing me to make some mistakes; and he didn't try to punish or bully me, he just sent me back out to finish what I'd started. I thought it was just him trying to make a point, trying to teach me a lesson. I guess he must have known that, because when I got off my horse he put his arm around me. We were right in front of our old log barn, a place they don't use much anymore at the ranch. It's just a place that holds a lot of good memories inside of it. I was tying my horse up to the front of the barn, and pulling my saddle off so I could take him down to the creek to pour water over him and wash all the sweat off. Forrest put his arm around me and said, "Son, I know that was hard on you and that horse to go back there and get those other three, but you need to understand why we have to do things all the way." He kept on, saying, "Buck, what if one of those older geldings that didn't come in was out there in the pasture caught up in the wire and he needed you to come get him out? Or what if he was sick or dying out there? You wouldn't want to be left out there. You'd want someone to think about you and count you. Even if you were too old to matter, where no one was going to ride you anymore, you'd still want to be counted, wouldn't you?"

Hearing that, I almost burst into tears. I felt sorry for those old geldings because they didn't get much attention anymore; they'd lived out their working life and were kind of retired. I looked up at Forrest, who finished by saying, "Son, I hope that when I'm like one of those old geldings, that you still count me, just like we counted them today."

This was just another lesson in life, but it was a big one. Forrest allowed me to work out the lesson at my own pace. I'm sure it goes without saying that I never wrangled horses again anywhere that I didn't get them all. We all matter, every one of us.

Just like me, Jean needed to learn to work things out and follow through, no matter how hard the lesson was or how long it took. She did, and as you'll see, the successes she's had with her horses speak for themselves.

JEAN'S STORY

I'm sixty-two years old and have had horses for about thirty years, but I've never been a very effective or confident rider. I owned and rode horses that were green-broke, and because of my lack of skills, I was bucked off and run away with many times. Twice I've had horses fall down with me, and I have sustained injuries. So throughout the years, I have developed a bit of fear to go with my lack of confidence; but because I love horses and riding so much, I kept forcing myself to get in the saddle.

After these accidents I knew I had to do something, so I began taking riding lessons. The lessons helped me to stay on the horse better, but I still felt I was missing a lot because it just didn't seem like I was learning how to avoid the problems—I was simply learning how to respond to them.

I started riding Tennessee Walking Horses because I was getting older, and my injuries and my age made it more difficult for me to post the trot (you can sit to this breed's running walk). I rode with some wonderful people who also had Walkers, and one gal let me ride her beautifully trained horse, which taught me a lot. I felt so confident on her horses that I decided to buy one, a beautiful bay tobiano filly. My friend was a very accomplished horsewoman, and she trained my filly, doing all the groundwork with her and a lot of ponying out on the trail. When the filly was two years old, my friend started riding her on trails. I was very anxious to ride my filly myself. I was sure I could handle her easily, but when I started riding her, all of my insecurities and fears crept back whenever things didn't go well. I knew I was going to need a lot of help, and quickly.

I decided that winter to attend Buck Brannaman's clinic at Bay Harbor Equestrian Club in Michigan. Unfortunately, the clinic wasn't until the following fall, and I needed to start riding this filly again in the spring. Whenever my friend would ride her, the filly did wonderfully. She was always in the lead and always consistent with her gaits. She went by objects without any problem, and she was always well behaved. But when I rode her, we would be the last one in the line and would get so far behind, we'd have to catch up, which would cause a little anxiety on my part; I didn't want her to go too fast for fear she would start bucking or run away with me. I gave the horse absolutely no confidence, and I felt terrible about it. The more I rode her, the less confidence I had, and the more my fears frightened my poor filly. It got to the point where I was making excuses for not riding. My friends tried to encourage me and be supportive, but it reached the point where they knew they really couldn't do anything more for me other than ride the filly themselves—which wasn't what the plan was supposed to be.

I was left to try and work it out myself, but I couldn't. I got very depressed and was getting ready to give up, sell my horse, and call it a day. By this point, it was time for Buck's clinic, and I actually had to force myself to go. Rather than taking my filly, I took Little Guy, my trusty little Quarter Horse who hadn't been worked in about a year (he was actually being used as my driving horse). When we got to the clinic, Little Guy whinnied constantly for his stablemate. I was completely embarrassed because my horse clearly wasn't with me, and didn't seem to want to be with me. I thought, *This is a pretty shaky beginning.*

Buck spoke to us a bit, and gave us some exercises to do. I started working Little Guy, and some very interesting things began to happen. We were riding without bridles, just a rope around our horse's necks, and we were asking them to do a rein-back. I just couldn't get Little Guy to do it, and had become quite frustrated. I approached Buck and told him that I couldn't seem to get this exercise down. So he said, "Well, let me watch you."

I was trying to get Little Guy to back with the rope by seesawing back on his neck. He took one step and Buck said, "Okay, release." I pushed my hands forward and I thought I was releasing. Buck kept saying, "Release, release." I remember looking at him thinking, *I don't understand what you're trying to say. I already released. What is it that you want?* Buck just looked at me and said, "You're not releasing." I wasn't trying to argue with him, but I was sure I had released. He said, "No. You still have contact with him. This time, try it and think about throwing the rope away."

I tried it again, this time throwing the rope away. Little Guy answered me right away. It was such a breakthrough for me because I'd had such fears of getting bucked off and being run away with. I always thought I had good hands, but Buck showed me that I hadn't trusted my horse, that I was never releasing my horse, never giving him a break.

From that point on, things progressed quickly. Little Guy started responding immediately when I'd ask him to do something. I was finally in real contact with my horse—we were communicating! This is a horse that I could never get to soften his poll or relax his jaw and yield to the bit, but by the end of the clinic, all I had to do was touch the rein and he would back for me. At one point, I sat and I asked Little Guy to shift his weight back and forth, which he happily did without moving his feet. We were finally a team!

Back home, all kinds of wonderful things happened, because I came away from the clinic with confidence and with tools I could use to communicate with my horse effectively. I started to do the groundwork with my green filly, and I felt confident enough to take her on trails. With my confidence and my newly acquired abilities, I began to expand on what I'd learned at Buck's clinic.

Buck demonstrates at a ranch roping clinic. A trick roper all of his life, he has performed all over the world.

"The first time people lead their horses to me, I can tell a great deal from their body language and the way their horses present themselves through their owners." (photo © 1995 by Diane Longanecker)

Except as indicated, all photos courtesy Buck and Mary Brannaman Collection

Buck calmly reassures a horse that he has just "laid down."

Starting a young horse from horseback enables Buck to safely work with his lariat.

Buck demonstrates the trust he can instill in a young colt, as the horse lowers his head into Buck's arms. (Photo by O'Brien)

"At first, the horse reared and struck at me, but by the end we had sorted it all out pretty calmly. You know, that little mustang just wanted a place to be safe—like we all do."

Country music legend Tanya Tucker watches Buck work her horse on her Tennessee estate. (Photo courtesy Patricia Presley Photography)

Buck travels over forty weeks a year and is away from his family quite a bit. Here Buck has a welcome chance to ride with his wife Mary, at left, at a Colorado clinic.

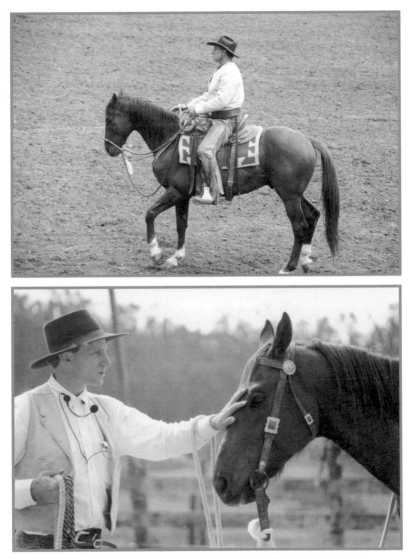

Buck and his "movie star" horse, Pet, who played "Pilgrim" in
The Horse Whisperer.

Buck at the OW Ranch. Buck feels that working with cattle really helps a horse find confidence. "Nothing helps a horse—or human—more than having a job to do."

*Buck instructing a
clinic student during
one of his numerous
visits to Australia.*

*Working with many
riders at the same
time can be daunting,
but Buck can foresee
problems as they
shape up.*

Mr. Brannaman Goes to Washington: Buck and family (from left, Lauren, Kristin, Reata, Buck, and Mary) visiting Washington, D.C.

Today, this filly and I are an incredible team; we're part-
ners. She bends around my leg; she listens. She's with me, and
she's such a joy to ride. I feel so good about myself that I'm
finally getting it, and I can't tell you how many people have
told me that they're impressed with the way I'm riding and
handling my horses. And it's not just my own horses. My good
friend, who started my filly out, has been allowing me to ride
her green horses that she has started out. All this experience
is translating to them also. They're softer and more responsive.
They're happy horses.

I purchased another Tennessee Walker from my friend, a
four-month-old palomino weanling named Annie. Right
after she was weaned, I started working with her, using the
tips and techniques I learned at Buck's clinic, and she has re-
sponded beautifully.

My friend and I planned to take Annie and two other
weanlings to a show, but before we went, we wanted to
make sure they would load into a trailer. So we put them
into the trailer and kept them loose, and then drove down to
a local lake to see if we could get them into the water for a
little bit of experience. When we parked at the lake, you
could hear the weanlings moving around, a little upset. I
called Annie's name, and all of the sudden her nose was right
at the side of the trailer, looking for me. We opened up the
door, and there she was at the front of the trailer. I called her
again, and she pushed past her two friends and came right to
me, letting me put the lead rope on her. We went down to
the lake, and when I waded into the water, Annie came right
in with me.

The biggest surprise came about a week after the show when I wanted to take pictures of her in her show halter and myself in my show attire. I had my friend hold her while I went into the house to change, and when I returned, my friend said that Annie had tried to follow me. When she wouldn't allow Annie to follow me, she started to whinny. My friend said, "I can't believe the bond that you have with this baby."

Thanks to Buck, I'm a much more patient person now, much calmer, more aware of things that are going on around me. I work as an executive secretary, so I'm used to a fast pace and the need to get my job done quickly and efficiently. I find that Buck's influence and wisdom have caused me to slow down at work and take a more relaxed, thoughtful approach to what I'm doing. I've also found that more and more people approach me and spend time talking to me, which hadn't happened before because I was so busy running here and there.

I am so thankful to Buck for everything that he has shown me and taught me. He has truly changed my life.

CHAPTER 5

BELIEVING IN YOURSELF

Reading these stories and preparing this book has been quite a process of discovery. Horses are not the only ones who reveal things about themselves at my clinics. I often say that given a few days with you and your horse, I'll make some discoveries about you that you probably don't want others to find out. For some strange reason, when people come to an arena full of horses and people, with a crowd watching them, they almost want to be discovered despite their attempts to cover up their fears. If you go to enough of these clinics, you'll soon realize that what's going on is as much about people working on their fears as it is about horses doing the same thing.

Fear can be projected in a lot of different ways. Some folks try to cover their fear by being pushy in a way that tends to make others want to push back. They can be equally aggressive toward their horse and anyone who approaches and tries to help by offering some constructive suggestions. Some people find all kinds of excuses why they don't or can't work with their horses, why they don't spend time with them, why they don't take care of their horses' needs. Some folks' fear even leads them to confront those who try to help them.

Some of the questions that Susan asked when she first attended one of my clinics seemed very confrontational. It seemed to me that she was grasping the things I wanted her to learn, but at the same time, she resisted accepting the fact that she just wasn't where she wanted to be—yet. As you'll see, Susan's horse was there all along, helping her learn things she needed to know about herself, including the realization that she had a drinking problem that was damaging her life and holding her back from the things she wanted to accomplish.

When someone like Susan shows up to be trained, and I sit down to supper to the end of the first day with the guys who work for me, I often hear comments like, "Boy, how about that lady who was asking questions there today? She was sure after you. It was like she wanted to pick a fight with you. What the hell was that all about?" Now, I've been doing this for twenty years, and when I hear things like this, I always caution people to hold off a bit. I find myself saying things like, "Don't make up your mind about someone the first day of a clinic." I've done that myself in the past, and I've been proved wrong more times than I care to admit.

Even though I think I've gotten better at what I do, I didn't start out that way. There was a time when I didn't believe much in myself or in what I had to offer. I'd find myself coming across as aggressive, or too ready to defend myself when I wasn't really being attacked. I then began to see that when I felt offended by something and felt like lashing out, it almost always had something to do with my feelings about myself at the time. If my self-esteem was low, so was my patience. Of course, some people would say that I've just mellowed over time because I have kids now, and I understand things from a different point of view. I do think time enters into it, but you don't just get older and more mellow like clockwork. It's not that simple.

I'm so pleased that what I do for a living helped Susan make this important journey of her own. I may not ever see her again, but I feel humbled that I was able to make a positive impact on her life. It's a responsibility I don't take lightly. I know that I'm never going to hit 100 percent and help everyone, but when I hear stories like Susan's, it just underscores the importance of my responsibility to be a good example and not to judge others too quickly.

Susan doesn't own horses now, but at this point in her life she doesn't need a horse around. She was lucky enough to have a horse come into her life and help her discover the things about herself that she needed to learn. At one point, that horse enbled her to hide and be reclusive and stop participating in relationships with other human beings, but by working with her horse, Susan found the loving, caring, tender part of herself that had been hidden for so long. Without that horse in her life, there may have been some loneliness in store for her; but it's clear that her old mare helped Susan to embark on a journey that will be a very fulfilling one for her.

SUSAN'S STORY

My life with Tallie was an amazing journey. It's often difficult to talk about her because I had her for so long, and I miss her. I got her when I was sixteen; she was two and a half then, and lived to be thirty-one years old, so we were together a total of twenty-eight years—more than half my life.

With all the publicity surrounding *The Horse Whisperer,* it was clear that this kind, gentle sort of horsemanship was going on all around me. My mom gave me a magazine article about Buck, and I became very interested in his method of working and communicating with horses; my horse was troubled to an extent, or I was troubled, or we both were troubled. I knew we had problems, but wouldn't have necessarily attributed them to myself at that time.

An opportunity came in May of 1998 to go to a clinic in Auburn, Washington. I was terribly frightened to go because this would be the first time I would publicly reveal anything about my relationship with Tallie. I knew that my horse was in many ways a mirror that reflected me, and as Buck says in his books, he can tell a lot about a person by working with their horse.

I had already owned Tallie for many years, and we both did everything wrong. If she ran away with me, I'd let her have her way. If I thought she was being pushy with me, I'd push her. She'd never hurt me, but the potential was there because I kept forcing her to do things. I didn't listen to her because it never occurred to me that she could have something of value to tell me. Besides, I was the one in control, wasn't I? Well, I knew she had bad habits, and I went to the clinic to get some tools that I could use to break those bad habits.

I had spent several years pulling back on Tallie to stop her, and even though it didn't work, I kept doing it because I didn't know there was another way. Buck made me realize that it wasn't my horse that didn't know how to stop—it was me who didn't know how to ask her to stop. He also made

me see that part of the reason I was yanking so hard was that
I had an inner fear that she wouldn't stop, that she'd run away
with me. There were many times she ended up with sores at
the corners of her mouth from my hard hands. And I kept
doing things that way, even though I was hurting her, because
it was safer not to admit I was doing something wrong. It was
safer not to put myself on the line and have to admit there was
something I didn't know. I think I had the feeling that, "Oh,
I'm in control, I can do this, I can push my way through. After
all, I've made it in life and a horse is just a horse." I didn't have
to learn anything new, and I wasn't willing to put myself on
the line and risk admitting that I wasn't perfect. What a concept! I thought I knew so much, but I've discovered that having that attitude is not only dangerous, but foolish. I have
found that there is so much more grace in life in being im-
perfect than in struggling to hide the fact that I'm not.

You can imagine how scary it was for me to even ask
questions at the clinic. But Buck was so kind and nonjudg-
mental; I soon learned new ways of communicating and connecting with Tallie, and grew less afraid to ask questions. I was
very inspired when I left that workshop, but I was jealous because I wasn't out there with my horse. The reason I didn't
bring her along was because I didn't think I was good
enough; I didn't think she was good enough; I didn't think I
had a right to be there.

I realized that I had been putting all these barriers in my
own way. I told myself I couldn't bring Tallie because I didn't
have a horse trailer. What about renting one? I wouldn't even
go there. I couldn't entertain that concept because I was afraid

of trailering my horse; or I didn't trust the people trailering, or I was afraid she'd fall through the bottom. I would dream up scenarios that would feed my fear and justify my failure to act, so the idea of getting her there became a nonissue.

I found out that I hadn't given myself or my horse enough credit. I thought she was incompetent because I thought *I* was incompetent. I was afraid of her getting out of control. I was afraid of being seen as incapable of handling my horse. My biggest fear was that people would think I didn't know what I was doing. I'd think, *Don't let anybody see me in that position because I'm supposed to have it all together. I'm supposed to know everything.* After all, at work I do a job that is very results-oriented, and I keep that together, right?

A long time ago when I was in my teens, I heard that someone remarked I was afraid of Tallie. At the time, I was indignant: "Oh, I am not. I ride her, how can I be afraid? I gallop with her." The truth is, I *was* afraid. I was afraid of what I didn't understand about her. I was always nervous around her. She jumped, I jumped. She moved, I moved. But I didn't understand the way she communicated her behavior at all. I regret now that I didn't go out and learn everything I could—but how could I? I was so afraid of her. I didn't go out and surround myself with other horsey people. How could I? I was afraid of people, too.

And so, having this unpredictable animal and being full of fears myself, I tended to keep away from others. I also kept Tallie away from other horses, which I truly regret, because she was a social animal and I know she would have loved spending more time with other horses. I just wasn't comfortable with people, so I kept her in places where I could spend time alone with her. Most people would probably say I'm a very social person, but the truth is, I was more myself when I was alone with Tallie than I ever was with other people. Because of where I lived, I always had to keep her in a place that was thirty or forty miles away so I only saw her on weekends. I know now that I was doing nothing to develop a real relationship with her.

Yet even though this isolation was bad for both of us, Tallie allowed me to have a relationship with her where I could more or less be myself, even though it was aggravating. I just couldn't understand why she ran from me when I tried to capture her. I'd think, *She's a bad horse. She's a meanie, she's spirited, she's the one with the attitude, not me.*

I had an image of myself as a mild-mannered woman, even though sometimes I would get angry with Tallie and hit her or kick her if I wanted her to do something. I would kick her until my legs got sore because as I told myself, Dammit, I want her to walk over that puddle! She's not going to get the better of me! I had a warped sense of competition with her. I'd think, *I'm in control and she's not going to get away with this.* But once I spent time in a Buck Brannaman clinic, I walked away with a new understanding of horses and their very special way of communicating. It's not about being big and forceful to get the horse to do what you want; it's about being clear but subtle. It's about being alive in the moment. I realized with horror that I had a wonderful creature with a wealth of experience and intelligence that I wasn't even connecting with.

I remember visiting Tallie the next day and just staying with her in her stall, something I had never done before. I was always at the barn to get something done, to accomplish something. I'd never experienced just being with her in a quiet moment. It turns out this was a thread that ran through my life: I never could relax. As a person, I didn't know how to just be in time. I've heard people say, "We're not human doings, we're human beings," but it never sank in until I met Buck. He taught me that I didn't have to be doing all the time. He taught me that accomplishing something with my horse was all about being with the horse. It's actually a relief to learn what it is to just be there.

It was eye-opening to learn how important groundwork is. Rather than just jumping on a horse and going, I discovered the benefit of being in the process rather than spending my time focusing on the end result. This knowledge really changed both my life and my horse's life, because I stopped going to visit Tallie with the idea that we're going to ride, we're going to do the trail, we're going to get this or that done today. I found out the real importance of simply walking with her, just putting the bridle on, or standing there quietly and comforting her. Simply being with Tallie, rather than demanding something of her, was a new concept for me. I had always felt that being with my horse was like a performance. I didn't understand that the learning was in the doing, the process, and the discovery, not necessarily in the outcome.

I soon relaxed around Tallie when I realized that I didn't have to do anything else when I was with her, that offering her comfort was learning, too. All along, I had thought I was doing her a favor by simply exercising her. I walked away from Buck's clinic knowing that there was much more to riding a horse than riding a horse. It's got to do with building a solid relationship with your animal.

Part of my fear was believing that Tallie didn't want me to touch her or be affectionate. Buck talks a lot about the comfort that a horse feels by being touched in ways that its mother would. I immediately started giving my horse lots of love on her neck when I was riding her, constantly reassuring her with my touch. I found her responding to me immediately with the release of pressure. Then I saw her relax, yawn, open her mouth, lick her lips, and give me gentle little taps with her nose, all of which she had never done before.

My ignorance and laziness all had to do with avoiding my fear. Every problem I had was my own, and the problems I had with Tallie reflected every other problem in my life. I know I'm not alone when I say that most of us try to construct our world; we manipulate the world and the people around us. We want the easy way out, and one way of doing that is to deny our fears. We step around our fears and avoid looking closely at what scares us.

There is a saying that "You are what you fear." I didn't want to be my fears. In taking steps to move through my fears, I began to see that those scary things out there weren't so scary after all. This realization has given me the opportunity to learn self-acceptance and self-love. Not surprisingly, when I felt those positive things about myself, they extended to my horse.

I'd kept my horse on pasture most of her life, and as a result, she became quite plump. I preferred not to notice that she was dangerously overweight (moreover, nobody told me to put her on a diet); I didn't want to restrict her pasture time, I told myself, because that would be sad for her to live on smaller pasture and not be able to run around. Deep inside, I knew that I wasn't giving her what she really needed in terms of attention, so I indulged her by letting her eat to her heart's content. That's not the way to love someone.

My generosity with Tallie, my patience and my understanding of her, all grew. In some ways, I began to see Tallie as a person, with as much intelligence as I had. I also stopped pretending that she wasn't a mature horse—an old lady if you will. She was twenty-five when I went to Buck's clinic, and so she was already a mature woman, but she was so generous. She gave me every benefit of the doubt. Contrary to what I had believed, she never held a grudge, and forgave me time and time again.

Following Buck's wisdom, my mind and heart opened to Tallie, and I became less stressed out. Going to see her on weekends, I had always had the idea that, "Oh my God, I don't have enough time to do this; but I've got to do this, so I've got to get out there. It takes forty minutes to drive out there, and now I've got to go catch her; I've got to do this and this and this . . ." I'm sure Tallie felt the tension rolling off me before I even got close to her. So I worked hard to stop doing that. I approached her slowly and quietly, and she stopped running from me. She approached me on her own and whinnied to greet me. It was a marvelous change in our relationship.

I also can't express how important it was for me to stop having foolish expectations and to stop demanding that Tallie be something other than what she was. It's a Zen way of being; not about having to be anything other than what you are right now. Buck taught me not to worry about something that hasn't happened yet; that serves no purpose.

As Tallie grew older, I began to question my motivations in terms of the rigors that I would put her through. I asked myself who I was doing it for: is this or that really for her benefit? Soon enough I realized that it was retirement time for her, so I allowed her to run in the pastures with other horses, free and happy and friendly in the company of two other geldings. These thousand-pound animals danced around as gracefully as butterflies, treating each other with such sensuality and tenderness. It enriched my life so much to see that side of her.

Eventually I accepted that I was going to have to put Tallie down. Her health was failing, with Cushing's, recurring laminitis, and other conditions. I looked hard at the quality of her life and said, "This isn't about me; it's about her. I can't keep this creature alive for my own pleasure anymore." I set up an appointment for the vet to come, but before that date, something happened and she went lame. We're still not sure how it came about, but I got a call from where I boarded her. I was told that Tallie's leg was terribly swollen and she was surely in great pain. When I got there, there she was, standing at the gate, waiting for me. Her leg was so huge, my heart just broke. But she had the love to softly nicker to me in spite of her obvious pain.

Putting Tallie down was terribly sad, but she was suffering so badly it had to be done. And the most beautiful thing happened after she fell. Animals came out into the pasture—black, white, brown coyotes—and then I heard an owl screech. To my thinking, they were welcoming her spirit.

Tallie continues to live in my heart, and I try to hold her generosity and her spirit close when I feel lost. I still don't know where my life will take me, but I try hard to be honest, and I keep asking for help from the Great Spirit in discovering what I'm supposed to do in this world. I know part of my journey was sharing a relationship with my horse. She was a great teacher. She never judged me; she always accepted me for who and what I was. Through her, and with Buck Brannaman's guidance, I learned to be honest with myself and others, and I discovered the wisdom in not being afraid of what's true.

One personal truth that I'd hidden for many years was my connection to alcohol. I always knew I had an alcohol problem. I drank too much; I drank when I didn't want to. For some reason, Buck's "Don't be afraid of what's true" lesson connected to my problem with alcohol. The day after Buck's clinic, I went for help. It's five years later, I haven't had a drink since. I am a changed person. I know that my quitting drinking had a positive effect on my relationship with my horse. I think I drank for the same reasons that I avoided training with Tallie: I thought I wasn't good enough, and I didn't love myself. I was always trying to be what other people wanted me to be, and I was certain, in my heart, that I wasn't even close. I was burying my feelings because I had been hurt. Well, I've made peace with the fact that life is not fair, because I've learned that we can grow in our capacity to love and accept.

My experience with Buck Brannaman was about more than learning to communicate with my horse. It was about softening myself and being willing to experience something different. I learned to accept the unknown and to trust that I can handle it. And you know what? I'm going to make it. I'll never be perfect, but Buck taught me that I don't have to be.

CHAPTER 6

LEARNING TO GIVE

I remember meeting Barb Jervis like it was yesterday. She had started one colt before she came to my clinic, but if you just listened to what she had to say on the surface, you'd swear she'd started hundreds of them. And because she was so nervous and so afraid, she did what a lot of people do—she just talked nonstop. I think when people are afraid or upset, they start going a mile a minute and they don't even realize it. At first, I found myself wondering if I would be able to teach this lady anything. I almost had to ask permission to speak because she was doing all the talking. But I came to realize that she was just a good-hearted gal, and was really concerned about doing things right. She definitely had a zest for life, and was up all the time—even though she was terrified that I might suggest she get on her horse.

In those days, Barb couldn't have ridden one side of that horse, the animal was so troubled. Yet she had great plans, and it was very discouraging for her to find out that I wasn't going to allow her to jump out there and try to prove something right off the bat.

Many of you will remember Nicholas Evans, the author of *The Horse Whisperer* and other books. He and I had just had breakfast, and we were talking about the notion of laying a horse down and how dramatic that scene was in the movie. The primary motive for Disney Studios and Bob Redford was to have the scene provoke some emotion, so folks would be upset when they watched it. And most folks do find it kind of upsetting, because they don't understand it. But laying a horse down is something I do with very troubled horses like Barb's that are inclined to buck their riders off and kick and strike at them once they're down, because these extremely frightened horses respond so well to it.

Laying a horse down looks like something that takes the life out of the horse, when really, it's a way to give him back his life. To get a horse to lie down, you have to put him in a situation where it seems to him that lying down is his only option. He's unsure of doing this, unsure about offering himself to you, because he's positive that if he's in such a vulnerable position, you'll take advantage of him. That's why you'll see a certain amount of resistance on the horse's part; but in a pretty short time, he'll lie down only to find out that you won't take advantage of him. In fact, his reward for lying down is your being loving and affectionate and respectful. That's a positive thing for everyone. The bottom line is that laying a horse down is really an act of love. Once he's down, he realizes that your reaction is to be soothing and affectionate and loving, which always comes as quite a surprise to the horse when he's in such a vulnerable position.

First, you put a rope around one front foot and wrap the end of that rope around the saddle horn. With one leg bound, the horse is forced to move around on just three legs. Once you get him moving around the corral on three legs and he learns how to balance his weight, he becomes less frightened of the situation and calms down a bit. At this point, you gently pull on the saddle horn at a 45-degree angle from the horse's hindquarters. As the horse attempts to drop his left shoulder, you release a little bit and ease up. Gradually, the horse will decide to lie down because he doesn't think he has any other options. As soon as you get him down, you give him praise and affection to help him overcome any fear he feels at being so vulnerable.

Once you allow him to get up again, you have a brief window of opportunity to accomplish more things with the horse, almost as if you put the horse's defenses in neutral for a few minutes. If you don't get anything accomplished within that next half hour or so, it'll all be for nothing, so you shouldn't waste the opportunity.

Laying horses down isn't something I normally do, but I did it with Barb's horse, along with using plenty of other techniques, to help build his confidence. It was clear that this horse feared for his life. I never did learn much about that colt's history, but there was no question that he'd either been poorly treated or badly frightened. Every horse that comes into a clinic has some history, no different than every human. You never figure on hearing the whole story about a person right off the bat; the facts just trickle out over time. It's the same with horses. Every now and then we all reach an important turning point, and laying Barb's horse down was a turning point for both of them.

In the film, *The Horse Whisperer,* the change that the horse Pilgrim had to make was to occur more or less over the course of a whole summer on a beautiful Montana ranch, but in reality, I only had a four-day weekend to make it happen. (Interestingly enough, in the film it took pretty much all summer for the relationship between the characters played by Robert Redford and Kristin Scott Thomas to blossom into something. I told Redford one time, "You know, being a big star like you are, it's amazing it would take you so many weeks to get someone like Kristin Scott Thomas to fall in love with you. But in the meantime, I'll keep you busy working on the horses so it looks like you're doing something.") That's why I use such methods, but in reality, laying a horse down is really no different than getting a horse to the point where you can put a rope on his hind foot and teach him to give with that foot.

Learning to give is a very important life lesson for all of us. I often remind people that if their horse ever gets caught up in wire, it just might save his life if he knows how to give rather than resist, how to relax rather than fight. Without having been shown how to give, it's quite possible that your horse could get cut so bad you'd have to put him down. And aren't the qualities of giving and patience and acceptance the same things we're looking for in our relationships with humans? If we could only learn how to yield rather than resist, to give rather than take, to put timid, frightened people at ease with calm assurance and patience—what a different world this would be. The bottom line is, when others trust you, they respond to you. It makes no difference if it's a horse or a dog—or a child.

The idea of giving and nonresistance is something I now share with far more people than just horse owners. I speak to audiences filled with corporate executives and temporary workers, athletes and couch potatoes, and all sorts of everyday folks who are just trying to raise their children well. In my opinion, raising a child is the most important job there is, and I'm very happy to be able to share this important teaching tool. To be successful in life, you have to know when to let go, when to give. I expect a lot of folks with kids will read this book, and I hope they realize that the rules apply to children just as they do to horses. It's all the same.

BARB'S STORY

I first heard about Buck Brannaman from a neighbor, an experienced hand who grew up with some well-known and highly respected horsemen and horsewomen. She told me about a Montana cowboy who was coming to our California town to conduct a colt-starting and horsemanship clinic. Ever since I was a young girl, I had a deep desire to understand how a horse thinks, and to learn how to better communicate what I wanted to accomplish in a way the horse could understand. I felt that what I was taught and what I knew weren't enough. It seemed to me that there were crucial pieces missing in how we represented ourselves to our horses.

These were thoughts I often pondered over the years, but I never expected Mr. Brannaman or anyone else to provide the answers. I decided to go to Buck's clinic because my husband and I had purchased a colt that was finally ready to be started. Even though I had started one horse on my own, I thought this would be a fun place to accomplish my first ride on him, and I was also hoping to learn some new things. So off I went, not expecting anything particularly profound or life changing.

However, by the end of the clinic, it felt like someone had given me a complete instruction book on horse–human relationships. Buck totally and completely understood horses. He knew how to communicate with them on a deep, instinctual level. He accomplished so much in such a short amount of time. When I was young, I dreamed that working with horses would be like this, but as I grew up, I never thought it could actually be accomplished. I was so excited about what I had learned that I wanted to share my new knowledge with everyone.

I quickly found out that many horse people didn't feel the need to broaden their education, and I soon discovered the wisdom of never offering advice unless asked. When someone did ask for help, they would only do so when they were at the end of their rope. Even though I barely knew anything, what I did know was far more fitting for the horse, and

I did have some success. Soon people began asking me to help them load their horses into trailers, or for help with other problems. As I dove into my newfound career, I was full of confidence. That all changed when a very special horse named Shredder came along that quickly humbled me and taught me some great lessons.

I took Shredder to one of Buck's colt-starting clinics in Ojai, California. I thought the problems I was facing with this colt could easily be fixed at one of Buck's clinics, but I soon realized I was in way over my head. We watched Buck lay my horse down, and although Buck tried to teach me how to do it, I was not capable of that kind of timing and skill. Buck explained that to get along with this horse, I would have to do six months' worth of perfect groundwork before I could even consider safely riding him. I was so depressed after that clinic that I just wanted to give up. I knew that I couldn't do perfect groundwork—or perfect anything, for that matter. I didn't know what to do with my horse.

I asked Buck if he knew anyone qualified enough to help me. He told me he knew of only one such man in my area—Brian Neubert. Brian worked with Shredder, and when we went to pick him up from Brian, he was gentle enough for us. Meeting Brian also had a profound impact on my life and on my family. We watched how Brian and his family treated each other, and I remember so clearly how this affected our family. I didn't realize what it was about his family that was so special until years later; their secret is, they all love God and each other, and they treat everyone they encounter—man or beast—with that same love.

My whole life has changed because of the things Buck has taught and shown me. My relationships with horses have improved dramatically. It is an awesome feeling to know when a horse appreciates you, when it's clear that he knows you know how to communicate with him.

As a result of learning more about horses, my husband and I started a horse transportation business that began from my being asked to load and move horses that other people couldn't manage. We also started buying and training horses, learning from them and training them before selling them and sending them off into the world. For a few years I spent time starting colts and helping people with their horses, but as the years progressed, we focused more on working for ourselves. Today, we limit our business to transporting horses and buying and selling gentle trail horses.

Other things in my life are drastically different as well. I see people and animals differently. I have learned to try to focus on the good aspects and overlook the negative ones. I have noticed that this always brings out the best in people, as well as in horses. Many of the problems we face with the horses that we've bought just melt away with a little effort. I sometimes forget a horse even had the problem. My husband and I have grown much closer as a result of our common interests, as has our entire family. When he and I used to load a problem horse, we would argue and disagree. With Buck's patient instruction, we realized that this sort of behavior would never get us very far. We've learned that everything goes much more smoothly when we work together. We've learned to have faith in each other and faith in God.

As I grew in my faith, the importance of calm understanding took on an even deeper meaning in my life and for
my family. Our lives are so rich with love and appreciation.
We have learned so much from each other, and as I continue
to learn about life, I think of it as an onion, with endless new
layers of understanding, each revealing more and deeper
meaning than the last. The more I discover, the more I realize
how much there is to learn. I think of my teenagers and how
sure they are that they know it all. But the older we get, the
more humble we should become, as we see more and more of
the big picture. Years ago, someone told me that horses will always tell the truth, and I never really understood that until
Buck showed me the full meaning. Horses don't lie. There are
no hidden agendas, just pure truth.

CHAPTER 7

MAKING THE RIGHT THING EASY

I'm often asked, particularly by the media, "How smart are horses?" I tell them that it's usually people who are a bit insecure about their own level of intellect who ask that question. (Hot-dog media folks tend to be taken aback at that response.) The truth is that I've never found it useful to spend any time worrying about how smart a horse is (or for that matter, a dog or a pig), because the things I teach my students about interacting with their horses are the same rules that apply to interacting with humans. You should treat a human the way you'd like him to be, rather than the way he is. The same is true with horses. I treat the horse the way I'd like him to be, not the way he is. There may be a lot of undesirable things happening, and there may be a lot of reasons why, so if you encourage the right behavior and don't respond to the wrong behavior, eventually the right behavior is what you'll end up with.

Ray Hunt once said, "A horse is multitudes of actions and reactions, separate and inseparable, all at the same time." I didn't make that up, but it really does define a horse. Since we humans made up the term "intelligence," obviously humans are going to come out on top in that contest. But because horses really are multitudes of actions and reactions, separate and inseparable, all at the same time, you're going to have to be pretty smart to deal with such a complicated creature. Often, when people ask me how smart or how dumb a horse might be, I think back to what one of my teachers said; "Well, I don't know how smart he is, but he's smart enough to out-fox you." That usually slows them up a bit.

It's important when working with horses to make the wrong thing difficult and the right thing easy. That's a philosophy I grew up hearing, and it really works. But be careful not to make the wrong thing completely impossible, because the horse has to have the opportunity to make the mistake in order to learn the lesson. You have to allow horses to search for answers and make their own decisions, and if they make a bad decision, you make corrections. However, it's important not to punish a horse for making a bad decision; we humans have a big responsibility to guide our horses to the right actions and to correct the wrong ones with respect and kindness. We also have to be ahead of our horses at all times, to shape things so they can make the right decision without difficulty or fear. As I pointed out earlier, but it bears repeating, this philosophy doesn't apply just to working with horses. You could just as easily switch the word "horse" with "human" or "child," and it's all the same.

Remember the mantra, "Observe, remember, and compare"? I counsel my students to observe what is taking place right now, remember what took place in the past, and then compare the two. Say you're trying to get your horse to learn some specific lesson. You approach the lesson the same way ten or fifteen times in a row. If the results each time are not the results you're looking for, you must adjust your actions to get your horse to respond differently, to get him to respond the way you want him to. So it's important to observe the results of what you've done, and especially to remember which actions prompted which results. When you compare the results, you're better able to hone in on exactly the right thing that will get the point across to the horse, always being careful to allow the horse to define the solution that works best for him.

This process works when teaching even the smallest of lessons. Perhaps you have to fight with your horse to get a bridle on him. Using this technique will help both of you find the best way to get the job done, with the least amount of stress or upset for both parties. Does your horse flinch each time you pull the bridle over his ears? Does he resist taking the bit? Observe what makes him react negatively and work around it to achieve the results you want.

To help my students achieve their training goals, I'll often advise them, "Do less than what you think it's going to take to get the job done." I mean that just the way it sounds.

Do less than what you think it's going to take to get the job done. Then, if you don't get the job done, build up to the point that you're doing *only* as much as it takes, and nothing more.

This idea confuses some folks when they first hear it, so let me explain the philosophy behind it: Sometimes people will do a little more than what it takes to actually get the job done, and they'll end up causing the horse to resent them or be cranky or disrespectful. You don't want to push the horse into something; you want him to go willingly. You're trying to offer the horse a good deal, and it should be offered with a happy heart. If he doesn't respond properly with minimal guidance, then it's time to become a bit more firm, to see if he responds to that. You slowly inch your way up that ladder until you reach the point where the horse responds properly, and that's when you and your horse get to celebrate a great victory. But always remember that this success is the horse's, not yours. You benefit in the horse's victory because you're on his back, but if you let the success be his, you'll be amazed at what he'll offer you in return.

AMY'S STORY

A few years ago, I picked up an eleven-year-old Quarter Horse-Arabian cross at a sale. He was quiet enough the day of the sale (I suspect he had been drugged), but by the time I got him home, he was skittish and uncontrollable.

When I was able to track down the woman who sold me the horse, she admitted that she hadn't been able to handle him. She had called in a trainer to cure the horse of his habit of rearing, and the trainer's solution was to pull the horse over backwards. Previous owners also had difficulties with the horse, so by the time I got him, he was angry and frightened of people.

Working with the horse had become a real test of wills. He was strong and stubborn and smart, and he fought me at every turn. I'd never dealt with such a difficult animal, and I was growing more and more afraid of him. His trust had been shattered, and everyone I knew asked me what I was doing with such an impossible animal.

After about a year of trying to work with the horse, I was close to giving up on him, when I heard about a man named Buck Brannaman who was putting on a clinic in a nearby town. People told me that Brannaman really knew how to change a horse's bad behavior into good, so I decided to check it out.

His clinic was held at a fancy equestrian center used primarily by English riders. I'll be honest and say that the setting and atmosphere put me off a bit, being a small-time horse owner with a Western pleasure background. Then I saw Buck looking like he'd just walked out of the Wild West, talking horses with a group of these fancy folks, and they were all listening intently.

Buck worked with a beautiful six-year-old Tennessee Walker that had similar trust issues to my own horse, so I watched and listened carefully to what he did and said. Buck said again and again: Horses that act out are generally doing so because they're afraid or nervous, not because they're intent on hurting or scaring humans. He repeatedly identified the frightened behaviors that the horse was exhibiting so those of us watching could recognize that the horse was just reacting to his surroundings the way a horse should. He made it clear that expecting a horse to react like a human is foolish. That horse must have been listening too, because after just a little while, Buck connected with that horse and it began to trust him.

That was the first time I had looked beyond my immediate, annoyed reaction to my horse's bad behavior and started thinking about why he did the things he did. I began to evaluate my horse's behavior in horse terms, and not in human terms. I went slowly, trying not to bite off more than I could chew, making sure that I was being safe as well as smart.

Don't get the idea that I just walked up and took charge; my horse was smart, but he had been taught to be afraid of people, to fight them. I had a lot of work ahead of me, but now I had the right tools to make some positive changes in both my horse and in myself.

Buck gave me a new respect for horses, and for people, too. Watching and learning from him helped me develop wisdom and patience that I hadn't had before. Buck taught me that, as much as we might love our horses, they need more than love from us. They need solid and patient instruction. They need reassurance and trust. They need someone who can understand where they're coming from. It's a learning process that you just have to keep working at.

My horse trusts me now, and I can tell that he knows everything I'm thinking. Probably the most important thing I learned from Buck is that I have to get my own head right before I work with my horse, because if my horse thinks I'm not paying attention or that he's cowed me, he'll try to take over. I have to be 100 percent centered when I interact with him, and I've found that this type of concentration works not only with horses, but also with people. If you can just stop re-acting to those around you and look more closely at where they're coming from, and why, it's much easier to deal with them effectively. Using Buck's methods in all aspects of my life has been a real eye-opening and very positive experience.

It's been three years since I attended my first Buck Brannaman clinic. In that time, my horse and I have slowly but surely built trust and understanding between us. He no longer feels as though he has to fight me all the time. He doesn't get confused or angry anymore. He's willing to keep working at a task till he gets it right, without turning every-thing we do into a test of wills. The level of concentration re-quired to work effectively with him has given me new powers of observation and interaction in all areas of my life, and al-though we still have room for improvement, we're both more calm and confident and effective. There's no question that my horse's trust in people has returned, and I attribute it all to Buck's brilliant teaching.

CHAPTER 8

FIGURING IT OUT

Val and Don are two really wonderful people who have been going to my clinics for quite a few years. They tend to be very quiet; they'll attend a clinic and you might not hear a whole lot from them the entire time, yet it's clear they're enjoying it as much as anybody could. Val and Don don't have to be the center of attention or be bragged on all the time in order to feel like they're getting something out of my clinics, even though they are. It's certainly noticeable, because their mules and horses are as good as anybody's. It does my heart good to be able to read about some of the things they've discovered, and I sure appreciate the cute story about working with me at my ranch. I have to say, I enjoy giving folks a job that's difficult for them and watching them work at it till they figure it out. I've learned that, if they don't get the job done, it's a bad idea to try to do it for them. Just like with horses, you have to let them make their own mistakes, and trust them to figure it out in their own time.

I was recently in Helena, Montana, giving a speech for the Child Services of the State of Montana in front of around five hundred social workers from all over the state, talking about raising kids and taking care of kids who are at risk. I shared my thoughts with the audience, about what I think is the right direction for kids to go, and how important it is for them to have a job to do. "I don't know why everybody is so afraid of hard work," I said. "And I don't know why people think that teaching a kid to work is abuse of some kind. As far as I'm concerned, not teaching a kid how to work and have some responsibilities is abuse." So many kids are so far behind when they're eighteen, nineteen or twenty years old because they've never really worked a day in their lives.

It's no different if you let a horse get some age on him without ever having had a purpose, never having had a reason for being. It never fails that he'll be the hardest one to work with. I often tell people that if you have a horse that's been on welfare for an extended period of time, and then you ask him to come off of welfare, he's going to resent you. He's going to resent being asked to go to work and have a purpose. Well, it's no different with some human beings.

VAL AND DON'S STORY

We have a dear friend named Chuck that we ride with every year at an event called Mule Days. Over the years, we've watched him ride his colts and his riding mules, and his exceptional horsemanship skills have always made an impression on us. Every year we'd see his mules improve and stand out above the others in the show ring. While other competitors were riding around with draw reins and gimmicks and all sorts of other things that made their mules uncomfortable, unhappy, and stiff, Chuck would glide around the arena, his mules showing a happy expression even while doing reining or cow-working patterns. Every year the question came up; "What's your secret? How did you do that?" We asked him a thousand times, and I'm sure he got tired of it, but the answer was always the same; "You need to go ride with Buck Brannaman."

We had a mule colt that needed to be started, so when Buck finally held a clinic in our area, we decided to attend. Being from the old school, Don wasn't sure he'd ride in the first clinic, but he wanted to watch. Buck was doing a five-day clinic, and it must have snowed four of the five days, but we were so intrigued by watching and learning from Buck that we stayed out there in the cold arena all day for fear of missing something.

That first clinic was a real eye-opener, not only for the excellent information we gained, but also for the feeling of excitement and discovery of how soft a horse could be—how you could set things up for the horse and really feel him looking for you.

Since then, we've attended other Brannaman clinics. At one ten-day clinic where both of us were starting colts, we were out in the pasture gathering some cows to bring back for the afternoon roping session. Buck needed a couple of the students to go to a small pasture by the arena to cut out a few head that we'd rope that afternoon, as well as to hold the other cows in the corner and open the gate so that Buck could add cattle that he was bringing back from another pasture. Buck sent the two of us and another student to get the job done.

We were up on a little hill, and as soon as we headed over the other side, all three of our colts didn't want to move.

We worked and we worked, it seemed like forever, all the way back to the arena to get them to move their feet, which made us pretty tired by the time we got there. Then we had to get the cattle cut and sorted, plus hold the others in the corner, before Buck and the group got back to the arena. We finally got the cattle moved over to the arena, and cut and moved about ten head through the gate.

One of the steers in front was holding up traffic, so Don rode up to push him forward a little bit. He then swung the gate closed, but didn't latch it. Just about that time a gust of wind came up and blew the gate back open. The cattle spotted the escape route and turned around and headed back out. Suddenly, another gust of wind blew Don's hat off. Perfect timing! It scared the cattle back in the pen—a great save. We got the cattle in and shut the gate, got them sorted and in the arena, and then hurried back over and held the others in the corner.

Don opened the pasture gate at just about the same time Buck and the others came up over the hill with their cattle. We all acted like everything was cool, but our hearts were going a hundred miles an hour. All three of us hoped to heck that Buck hadn't been sitting on top of that hill watching us scramble around.

The point of this story is that the whole time we were working at getting this job done, and trying to do it right, we were doing it for Buck. Buck's quiet honesty has a way of making everyone who meets him want to work extra hard to get a job done—and done right—for the benefit of both rider and horse.

Don wrote a little something that we want to share with Buck and his readers:

I sat on the fence quite a few years before I finally decided to enter up. I regret that it took me so long. Val kept telling me I really needed to go ride with Buck; it was different than watching, and I could come away with so much more. So I signed up.

I had a mustang that I wanted to do something with. He was coming along pretty good, but something was missing. He seemed to be boogered about a lot of things. I was having trouble with my groundwork; I couldn't get what I was looking for fast enough. I asked things of my horse and didn't know why they wouldn't happen, couldn't figure out why it was so difficult. Patience was not one of my virtues.

Well, Val was right. (She wanted me to put that in.) I learned so much from Buck at that first clinic, and my little mustang was sure thankful. Buck was able to see my frustration, and he helped me work through it to benefit both my horse and me. I didn't work on having more patience; it's just that because of what I've learned from riding with Buck, I seem to automatically have more patience. That alone has made a great impact on my life, my horses, and my health. I'm a better person, for sure.

CHAPTER 9

BAD THINGS
AND GOOD PEOPLE

What can I say about Sissy? After reading her story, you'll understand what I mean when I say she's a very special lady. She showed up at one of my clinics and seemed so unsure of just coming up and saying hello. I also remember how relieved she was to discover that I was friendly, as if I was going to be any other way. But at the time I didn't know her, and I had no idea of the burdens she has had to bear. She's had more trouble with her health than anyone I know; she continues to decline, but she has a great spirit, and as much try as anybody. Sure, she gets discouraged, but that's what friends and family are for, isn't it? Going through her personal troubles, Sissy has found out what a wonderful family she has. Her kids and her husband are special people who really care for her. Many folks who are sick don't have that kind of support to rely on.

About two years ago, we were filming a pilot for a television series—sort of a reality series that would follow me around to clinics and tell the stories of people who come and go in and out of my life. Some would be personal stories about human relationships, and some would be about horses. Well, Sissy came to mind as one of the stories for the pilot because of the challenges she's faced in her life with multiple sclerosis, cancer, and it seems every other thing under the sun.

I called Sissy up about being a part of this pilot. She said, "You wouldn't believe me if I told you what I was doing just now when you called." Since she didn't tell me during that phone call, I got the idea that she didn't want me to know, and I didn't press it. But after reading her story here, I now know what was happening in her life at that moment. She was in crisis.

I haven't talked to Sissy for a couple of months. I'm always afraid that when I go back to Texas, I'll find that Sissy is no longer there. But somehow, I have an idea she's going to hang in for a while. And if spending a few days a year with me at a clinic helps give her a reason to stick around a while longer, I'm glad to be there.

Because I meet so many people in what I do for a living, I end up hearing about a lot of despair and terrible trials that people have to deal with, whether it's cancer or some other health problem. Sometimes it just about sucks the life out of me because I feel so bad for these really good people. It's like the old saying goes, "Bad things happen to good people." Bad things don't seem to happen that often to bad people. It's sad that so many really terrific people have to deal with really terrible obstacles; troubles aren't always based on what people deserve.

At some point in our lives, we all have our turn at despair. That's why, when things are going well, it's important to appreciate them. If your horse didn't change leads, if he didn't stop perfectly or turn around the way you wanted, is it really that big a deal? To me it's not. I'm simply happy to have the opportunity to be able to work with a horse and enjoy him and enjoy being a part of him. You know, I've seen the other side. Those of you who have read *The Faraway Horses* understand where I'm coming from; you know that I've seen the ugly side of life. So I try to follow the wise advice: "Don't sweat the small stuff." I don't. I used to—but not anymore.

I think that with some of the things I do in my work— some of the things that I say, the places I go, the people that I take time to visit with—I'm just being used by the powers that be: God, Jehovah, Allah, whatever you want to call it. A supreme being is directing us, if we would just listen. And my role in this life may be to be used in a manner that hopefully does some good for others.

I don't know that I've done as much good for Sissy as she's done for me—as far as inspiring me to try to be a better horseman and a better person—but I do care about what happens to her and to the others I come in contact with as I wander through this life. My making that phone call right when she needed it convinces me a greater hand is guiding all of us.

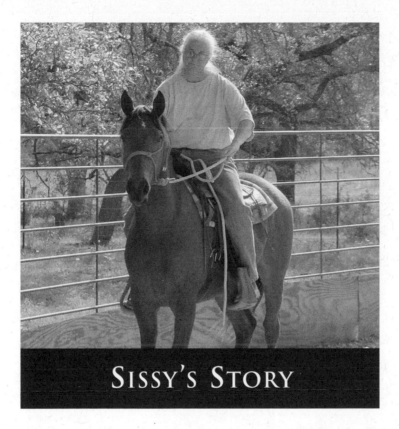

SISSY'S STORY

I believe that nothing happens without a reason, and little by little, I keep seeing what that reason is.

Because of my medical problems, I hadn't felt well enough to ride a horse for some time. I thought my life with horses was over. I love horses—I have all my life—so not being able to ride had become so painful to me, I couldn't even watch Westerns on television. Why watch something that made me feel even worse?

Nevertheless, I have always subscribed to a magazine called *Cowboys and Indians,* one of my favorites. A while back, an issue had an ad for a book called *The Faraway Horses.* It sounded like something I might like to read. Now, you must understand that I'm not much of a reader, but this book caught my eye, so I ordered it.

Once *The Faraway Horses* came, I couldn't put it down. I finished it within a day or two, which is quite an accomplishment for me. I couldn't stop thinking about the book, or about Buck Brannaman. Everything about him intrigued me: where he had come from, what he had accomplished, his goals in life, and his attitude in general.

Hoping to learn more about Buck, I went to his Web site and found out that he was scheduled to do a clinic in San Angelo— the only one he does in Texas—in a few weeks. I told myself, "I need to go to this if at all possible." More than likely, I wouldn't even get a chance to meet the man, but I wanted to at least see him, to prove to myself that he did truly exist. His picture was in his book, but sometimes I can't help the skepticism that I've developed through my life.

I'm fortunate to have a very supportive husband, who said, "You're going to go. However it has to happen, we'll get you there." So I packed my bags, and with butterflies in my stomach, I took off for San Angelo.

I got to the clinic early because I wanted to get a good seat. There wasn't a very large crowd, which surprised me, but that didn't really matter: I was there to see Buck. Then a man came into the arena without fanfare. There were no whistles blowing; he just rode his horse into the arena, introduced himself, and started telling the attendees how the class would go. He then proceeded to work on these horses; or rather, he worked *with* them—weaving his magic with his kindness toward the animals, and his understanding and patience with the folks in his clinic—some of whom would try anyone's patience (I know they would have tried mine). Yet I never saw the man lose his temper or act frustrated.

Buck did something that I had never heard of before, and I've been around horses all my life. He called it groundwork. What Buck and the horse he was working with did was like an elaborate dance. He would make a suggestion for the horse to move forward, maybe move in a circle from his left to his right. Then Buck would direct the horse to move his hindquarters to the left and bring his front across to the right. The result was like watching two talented dancers glide across a ballroom floor with effortless grace. Of course, horses can be afraid of new situations, and will be uneasy about having a human decide where they're going to put their feet; but through the course of this groundwork, Buck took a frightened, uptight horse and literally danced with him across the arena. Buck moved his hind and front ends, moved him forward and back, rubbing the horse, praising him, touching him in areas that the horse isn't normally inclined to allow himself to be touched, all the while preparing him for things that are going to be a part of his future, and making him feel so safe that you could put a saddle on him without him tensing up at all. Ultimately, Buck had such control of the horse's feet—in a willing way—that if Buck didn't ask the horse to move, the horse felt as if he had nowhere to go. It was like watching Fred Astaire and Ginger Rogers out there.

It doesn't take me long to size up a person. Reading about someone is one thing, but when I can see someone in action, I can see things in their eyes and hear things in their voices that carry a deeper meaning. A person's actions all mean something, and what really impressed me about Buck was how he dealt with animals and people alike with gentle respect and dignity. People would ask questions and he would help them, and they would say "Thank you," and Buck's answer was the gentlest, most sincere "You're welcome" I've ever heard. It didn't just come from his mouth; it came from his heart.

When you sign up for a Buck Brannaman clinic, you'd better be ready to work, because that man doesn't stop. He seldom gets out of the saddle unless he's helping someone with his or her horse. Buck works the morning class, breaks for lunch, and when it's time for the evening class, he's Johnny-on-the-spot. He does not leave the arena until the class ends. That's when he stops working, and sits quietly in his trailer, usually smoking a cigar. As much as I didn't want to bother him, I just had to speak with him personally, so before I left his clinic, as nervous as I was, I went up to Buck's trailer and knocked on the door frame. I had nothing to be afraid of, as it turned out. He couldn't have been nicer to me, could not have made me feel more welcome and more comfortable, as if I were an old friend he'd known for life. His talent for putting animals at ease worked just as effectively on humans.

When I returned from that first clinic, my mind raced. There was so much to remember, so much to think about. I went home and read *The Faraway Horses* two or three times more, and since then I have given out many copies. I'm not a wealthy person, but I want people to see the message that's in there. I tell them, "If you read the words, it's a good book; but if you really listen to them, that's where the true message is—and that message doesn't necessarily have anything to do with horses."

My life seemed to take on a new sparkle, to hold more promise. I had much more energy—not something I usually have a lot of—but now I had a goal and it kept me going strong. My husband had asked, "What did you think of the clinic?" I replied, "Oh, my gosh. It was just wonderful, and now I've got to buy a horse!" He stepped back and said, "A horse?" "Yes," I said, and my wonderful husband said, "Then let's do it." My two sons chimed in and said they wanted to help with whatever we needed done.

I wanted a horse that was not broke. Hearing that, most folks would look at this fifty-something-year-old woman and say "What kind of medication is she on?" But my husband and my sons saw my excitement and determination, and everyone pitched in. They built me a riding ring and all the pens I needed, right where I can look out from my bedroom and see my horses even when I'm too tired to ride them.

Not long afterward, I took off to look at a little gelding that was for sale. Well, I bought him and started working. I was so pleased with how it went. Everything I did worked—I was on cloud nine. And even though I knew I should never get on a horse again because of my poor balance, I couldn't resist after working this colt for a little while, so I slid on him bareback. He turned to sniff one of my boots and then the other; there are no words to tell you what that simple act did for me.

Well, time moved on and I got other horses. Buck Bran-naman's teaching and wisdom continue to have a positive impact on my life, in countless ways. There was a time when I had been receiving chemotherapy and I had not been out of bed in three months. I kept trying to go outside, if for no other reason than to pet my horses. One day, which happened to be my birthday, I made the effort and went outside. I fell twice on the way, and finally came back inside. I was gearing up to have a great big pity party when the phone rang. It was Buck Brannaman. To be quite honest, I had been lying there planning my funeral, and suddenly, there he was, lifting me up and inspiring me yet again.

I went to Buck's Texas clinic again the following year. My health had deteriorated to the point where I couldn't even get up into the bleachers, so I sat in a lawn chair on the ground for the first day. By the second day I was asking myself why I'd come. It seemed to me that I would never get near a horse, so I got up, packed my stuff, and was fixing to walk out when I heard Buck speaking with the rider he'd just helped. The rider thanked Buck, who said, "You're welcome. I will always help anybody who tries, but I won't help a quitter." That stopped me dead in my tracks. I turned around, put my stuff down, sat back in my lawn chair, and finished watching the clinic. And am I glad I did. I came away that day with even more knowledge, especially the fact that it's important to do what makes you happy. If you don't enjoy what you're doing, find something else that you do. And that makes perfect sense. So now, when I'm having a bad day, I think of Buck and how important it is to put your heart into everything you do.

I've often thought how many children could be helped, emotionally and physically, by having Buck give talks or exhibitions at their schools. His story is important. His message is important. I'd be thrilled if more people could hear it. It's really a shame that so many people look at Buck Brannaman and folks like him—Ray Hunt and Tom Dorrance, for example—and think they're just old cowboys. Well, no, they're not, not by a long shot. People hear the term "horse whisperer" and think it's all a bunch of mumbo-jumbo. It's not about whispering in a horse's ear at all. It's about how you treat animals, and by extension, how you treat others. If more people could hear this message and understand it, my goodness, what a difference it would make.

Today my health is declining a little more rapidly than anticipated, but I'm hanging in there, and that in itself is a good sign. Buck told me not long ago that maybe my life isn't over yet—that I do have a purpose—and although I'm still looking for that purpose, I know it's there somewhere. At least I have the joy I get from my horses and the thrill of all the wonderful things my family has done for me.

In a couple of days I'll be leaving for another one of Buck's clinics, and I know that even before it's over, I'll already be looking forward to the next one. Buck has shown me that you can do anything if you're willing to give it your best, and I'm proof of it. I know there are all sorts of similar stories out there about the things he's done for other folks, but I also know there are even more folks out there that need a Buck Brannaman in their lives.

CHAPTER 10

FROM HERD-BOUND TO INDEPENDENT

I met Nicole at my clinic in Tehachapi, California. The little black-and-white horse she rode in on looked like he had a lit-tle mustang in him. A lot of times that can prove to be quite a challenge for folks, because mustangs live and die by the flight response.

Nicole was a quiet rider and got along reasonably well with her horse. At one point I told everyone to lope their horses around the arena in both directions. This exercise helps riders find out exactly what's going wrong for their horses by moving at a faster pace, where problems are often amplified. Most folks work slowly through the walk and the trot and get them accurate, but when they begin to speed up, the problems pop right up and you can see them clearly.

As the class moved around the arena, I noticed Nicole wasn't having much luck getting her horse to lope on the proper lead. Proper lead refers to a horse's natural and balanced way of moving. It has to do with the sequence of feet hitting the ground. For example, when a horse is on his left lead, his left front and left hind legs reach farther forward in the stride than his right legs do. A horse that takes the right lead has both right legs reaching farther forward. Some horses, when out of balance or moving uncomfortably, will even crossfire—which means they could be on the left lead in front and the right lead behind. That makes for an incredibly rough ride; you'll feel like the fillings are going to come out of your teeth. And sometimes horses will be on the wrong lead completely, on the right lead while going to the left. That's called a counter-canter, and it can be dangerous because the horse can literally have no leg to stand on when making a sharp turn.

Nicole was having a hard time getting her horse on the proper leads, but I also noticed that her horse seemed to be somewhat distracted. He was motivated by being with other horses, which is known as being herd-bound.

When I ask at my clinics if there are any herd-bound horses in the bunch, one or two people might raise their hands, but all of them probably should. Horses aren't solitary creatures by nature; they like being around other horses, so it's not hard to see that most horses have at least a few herd-bound tendencies, no matter what. It's just that some horses are less herd-bound than others, and some riders are less aware of it than others. You often find a rider who doesn't recognize that the horse's herding instinct is what's preventing him from concentrating on the lesson. The rider thinks the horse has a problem with that particular lesson, and the underlying issue never gets properly addressed. Of course, we all know that a small problem can often affect a lot of other things, and if we don't do anything, it turns into a big problem. And because it's always easier to fix a small problem than a big one, I try right away to catch any herd-bound tendencies my students' horses may have.

I had everybody get in the middle of the arena, with Nicole and her horse to the outside. That's when she realized how determined this horse was to be near the herd. The big issue is not that your horse isn't going to the exact place you'd like him to go, but that the horse is completely shutting you out and has other things on his mind rather than being with you. The horse puts the human's wishes after his own, and with that comes a multitude of problems.

NICOLE'S STORY

There was a time when I couldn't even get on my horse,
Apache. My friends would all be mounted, ready to go on a
ride, while my little black-and-white horse and I would be
doing three-sixties around each other for twenty minutes before I could jump on and get under way. I got Apache from
a horse trainer in Bakersfield, and this horse had been
through quite a few owners; a total of about nine brands
ought to tell you something. I was never afraid of him,
though. He seemed to be more unsure of me than I was of

him. It was obvious that someone had done some pretty awful stuff to this horse, and since I wasn't going to give up on him, we were going to have to learn to get along. I made him a promise that he could stay with me and I wouldn't put him through any more hard times.

A neighbor told me about Dave Ferry, a horse trainer here in Tehachapi. I contacted him and made arrangements to be included in his clinics and training schedule. Over the next couple of years, my horse and I learned a tremendous amount together, and soon enough we started to build a real partnership. Dave would often mention Buck's name, and always spoke of him with the highest regard. He encouraged his students to attend Buck's clinics wherever and whenever possible, so when I learned that Buck was coming to Tehachapi in June two years ago, I started saving up so I could attend his clinic.

On the third day, we were working on loping to the left and loping to the right and making sure we were picking up the correct lead. Apache and I were having a problem picking up the left one. It just felt very strange to go around to the left, and Apache consistently picked up his right lead going to the left. I really struggled with this problem, and when Buck asked if anyone had any questions, I said, "It feels like he's pushing to the inside with that left shoulder."

Buck asked me to show him what I was talking about. I started out going to the left, while the other riders—some twenty-five to thirty of them—stayed in the middle of the arena. Just as we'd done before, I led Apache around to the left, and he kept picking up that right lead. Suddenly, Apache dove into the center of the arena where the other horses and riders were. Buck said, "Well, we're working on two different deals here. She's having trouble with that left lead, and the horse is obviously herd-bound." Then he hollered out to the crowd and asked if anyone had a night latch that I could borrow.

A night latch is a strap that runs through the pommel or the fork of a saddle. It's used as a handhold, and for someone with small hands, it's better than holding onto the saddle horn. You put your hand through that strap to stay more firmly seated on top of the horse. Buck's assistant, Kip, came out and put the night latch on my saddle, and Buck told me to drape my reins over the horn.

I was riding Apache that day in a hackamore with mecate reins. A hackamore is a type of bridle that loops over the horse's nose but has no bit to put in the horse's mouth. Mecate reins are made of one continuous piece of rope that attaches to both sides of the bridle, with a lead rope coming off of it that goes through your belt. The idea is that when you get off and on your horse, you've got a lead line right there in easy reach.

Buck told me to quit riding when my horse and I got to a specific back corner of the arena. When we were every place else in the arena, I was to stay busy, keeping the horse going, doing whatever I had to do to keep him moving. Buck also instructed everyone in the center of the arena to spread out a bit and make lots of noise every time my horse and I came near them.

Apache is very sensitive to pressure. If I'm on him standing side by side with another horse and rider, and someone tries to hand me a Coke while I'm on his back, Apache gets bothered and kind of flies off in the other direction. So every time Apache started heading toward the center of that arena and the other riders waved their arms and made noise, Apache wheeled and sped off at about Mach five in the other direction.

I thought we would never get back to the far back corner of the arena where I could just quit riding, but I could also tell my horse was really searching for the answer. He didn't want to fly around that arena at a hundred miles an hour any more than I wanted to, but he didn't know what else to do.

Keep in mind that my reins were draped around the saddle horn, and I was holding onto just the night latch. My legs started to feel like jelly, and my horse was wet from his ears to his hooves. I just about came out of the saddle as we flew around the arena for what felt like hours. In reality, we probably only spent twenty or thirty minutes at it—with Buck telling me to hang in there the whole time—but I was really running out of steam. I started having a hard time keeping Apache going. Every time Apache got a little closer to that corner, Buck told me to just be quiet and then reward him every time we were back there. But when I tried to, Apache would take off back toward the center again, and I and everyone else had to get busy all over again.

After what seemed like an eternity, we were finally standing in that back corner of the arena, but still, Apache took off toward the herd. We made our way back to the far corner of the ring, and I stayed quiet, and finally, Apache started to figure out that this was where he was supposed to be.

As happens when horses have been working hard, he was soaking wet by the time we made it back to that corner.

Buck told me to take the saddle and blankets off right there
and hang them on the arena fence, then take Apache out, hose
him off, give him water, and then come rejoin the others after
Apache and I had had a fifteen-minute breather. I got off my
horse and thought I was going to fall flat on my face. My legs
were rubber, and my knees hurt terribly because I had been
gripping as tightly as I could. (I ended up with a couple of
small holes along the seams of my jeans, and actually rubbed
my skin raw in a few places.) I really felt the effects of that
ride, but as I was taking Apache out of the arena, people ap-
plauded while others stood up and cheered. Suddenly my
aches didn't hurt as much.

Apache and I both worked ourselves into a lather that
day, but it was necessary to help him overcome those years of
resistance that had built up in him. All along, he'd been call-
ing the shots, but it was time for us to learn to work together,
and Buck made us both understand how to accomplish it—
by making the right thing easy and the wrong thing difficult.
It was truly a valuable lesson, and I have the scars on my knees
to prove it.

That hard ride that Buck put us through also gave me
an opportunity to learn how to ride with my horse, rather
than resisting him and trying to overcome his far greater
power and stamina. Buck taught me to go with the energy of
the horse, and I learned on my own the benefit of not gripping too tightly with my knees when I was afraid or intimidated by the horse. Not only did I learn how to ride better,
but Apache learned that he could go out alone with me and
still be safe. A horse that is so herd-bound that he'll fight you

to stay near other horses is dangerous for rider and horse alike, so these were important lessons.

Apache is confident when we go out now. He's not bothered about being away from other horses, and when we're in an arena, he's learned to stay close to the outside rail. We get along together on our own, and we've both grown more comfortable with that, even though we still have a way to go.

CHAPTER 11

THE SPIRITUAL PART

For some folks, this horse thing can be like searching for the Holy Grail. Some people just want to be safer and more confident on a horse, because they rightly believe that confidence gained through being able to maneuver a horse successfully will help them with some of the other things they encounter in life. But for other people it goes much deeper. The connection they make with a horse can be a genuinely spiritual thing that may even help them get closer to God. It's a different experience for every person, so I'm careful not to judge anyone at the beginning, or try to manipulate the outcome for them. Just like the work I do with horses, I'm not there to push; I'm there to guide and encourage and support.

Tom Dorrance, one of the greatest horsemen of a generation, told me, "Buck, it's all about feel, timing, and balance." And then he added one other thing: "and the spiritual part of your relationship with a horse." Of course, spirituality is a very subjective thing, a very private thing to each person. Diane's story reveals that spiritual connection between horse and human, and I'm pleased and honored to have been a part of it.

DIANE'S STORY

*I*t all began with *The Horse Whisperer*. I had no idea what an impact the movie would have on my life and that of my Arab gelding, Russic. The storyline was entertaining, and I was completely fascinated by the natural methods of horseman- ship that were demonstrated in the rehabilitation scenes with Pilgrim. It was very moving to see what could be accom- plished without gadgets and contraptions. Tom Booker's train- ing concepts appealed to me because I felt an overpowering identification with Pilgrim. I knew all too well what it was like to not have a say in how I was being treated. It was evident that a horse could hold a conversation with his handler, but the animal needed a willing ear, and the opportunity to not to be commandeered by man.

For days and weeks I tried to rationalize all the training that had been drummed into me, which taught me to stand up to the horse through fierce determination and dominance. Since I'm a very sensitive person, my emotions vacillated between that of a more passive leader, and guilt for blindly following the soon-to-be-outdated protocols of horsemanship. The prospect of letting go and trusting the horse's natural instincts only intensified my confusion. I wanted to formulate an image of myself not on top of a horse, but rather, within a horse—a communication of beings that I had begun to feel only recently. I would venture a guess that many of the people Buck meets have been subjected to the same faulty training methods I had experienced.

At the age of nine, I took my first English riding lessons at a large facility in Michigan. I would enter the riding arena and quickly mount whatever random horse I was given. Knowing its name was the extent of my connection. The message was clear: Leave your emotions at the gate. The arena felt very cold and impersonal. I wasn't taught how to ride, but rather how to manage a horse through dominance and/or pain. Though I loved horses, I knew of no other way than to kick, whip, and demand. I spent more time in the dirt than in the saddle, and my list of injuries grew. I thought that a head-shy or a crop-sensitive horse was the norm, because that's all I ever saw. The notion of feeling one with the horse was foreign to me. I'd create ground time to groom and interact on a more intimate level with horses, but something was still missing.

That's why at age eighteen, I chased my cowboy experience and spent three summers in Lake Louise, Alberta, Canada, doing trail rides for Brewster Stables. I rode for the right reason, to ascend rugged mountains and switchbacks in the company of nature. I opened my heart to days of sunshine, snow, and rain with my equine guide and companion. I felt emotionally intact with nothing more than my pony underneath me. I knew that I was finally on to something.

It was an honor to introduce greenhorns to the trail on horseback. Though we traversed rock slides and ice crevices, I never found a horse that was unwilling to do his job. With four legs they were able to teeter on the edge of air at six thousand feet, and these were not formally trained horses. Due to their number and circumstances, they were virtually green. They wintered in harsh mountain ranges and foraged on their own for food in order to survive. They knew their jobs, and since their passengers weren't micromanaging them, they willingly accepted their responsibilities and always came through for us. These horses even passed among grizzly bears and other dangers with predictable reliability.

Unfortunately, though, I had to wait years for a special horseman like Buck Brannaman to reveal deeper truths.

The first time I laid eyes on Buck was four years ago at his clinic at the Bay Harbor Equestrian Club in Michigan. He was in a round pen starting a young horse. A sense of calm permeated the arena; Buck exuded confidence and understanding.

It was very obvious that he intended to lay the foundation for equine success. He wasn't at the clinic to perform for an audience or to gentle a horse within a certain amount of time, and there was no fanfare or hype. Buck remained present with the animal that was looking for him to lead the herd, and I never heard him whisper once (which, of course, he doesn't really do). Buck didn't stand in the middle of the pen chasing the horse away; he waited for the twitch of an ear, or the glance of an eye, which indicated the horse was interested in him. Then they'd kind of dance with each other before the horse hooked on. Buck allowed the horse to move at its own pace, and as a result, the horse always wanted to come back to Buck.

When it was time to put on a saddle, Buck helped the horse feel a sense of herd by bringing his own horse into the pen. Then he went a step further by mounting his own horse and riding alongside the young one, so the green horse became acclimated to the sight, sound, and smell of a human being above him. Buck said that this step was very crucial because of the horse's position in the wild as a prey animal. Horses have to constantly be aware of any cats roaming in the vicinity, and their survival depends upon their ability to keep any wild cats off their backs. To them, a human is just another cat when we're on their backs. Buck knows that a herd communicates through body language, not the spoken word. On this particular day, Buck was thrown from the youngster, but, unfazed, he used this opportunity to share how a fall affects a horse. When a human is thrown from a horse's back, the horse doesn't immediately know where the human is, and thus fears that "the cat" could rebound and attack again.

Buck was next introduced to a troubled stallion. Its owner led it slowly down a long, grassy hill, all the time keeping the horse at bay with a long whip. It was obvious to Buck that the horse was inadvertently being set up for failure. The more the horse was provoked by the whip, the more defensive its owner became, and the more the horse acted up. The handler was more than ready to tell Buck her story, but Buck politely told her that the horse would tell him everything that he needed to know. In a very short, painless amount of time the horse became calm and compliant. As is so often the case, it was the owner had to be retrained.

The session that will forever remain in my mind was the one in which Buck helped a very troubled gelding whose handicapped rider had difficulty mounting the animal because of its size. While the horse was troubled for other reasons, Buck also wanted to show the horse how to comfortably lie down so that his rider could slide a leg over and ride him up.

The moment the horse was led into the round pen, my emotions resonated with him. I identified with his need to trust and to be trusted. Once more, Buck took his time to reassure the gelding. Slowly, the horse showed signs of releasing stress. When it was time, Buck carefully helped the horse lie down in the sand. The horse stayed focused on Buck, who very gently soothed and stroked his tense body. With each stroke, the horse fell into a deeper trance, totally unaware of anything else. Then, in a rhythmic mantra, the horse gave out sighs and moans as Buck helped him dispense with his traumas and abuse. Buck shared with the audience that the horse had endorphins flowing through him, and that he was in no hurry to rise to his feet.

Tears of pure emotion streamed down my cheeks. Here was a man who, in spite of his very difficult and painful upbringing, allowed his sensitivity to be seen, and encouraged others to do the same. He extended his trust to what was deemed a crazy horse, and it was reciprocated. My very core had been reached; it felt safe, and I let it open up. I would never, ever interact with a horse in the same way. I wanted to be like Buck and feel confident and self-assured.

The last four years since my first clinic have been filled with personal growth both inside and outside the arena. The inspiration from those few days with Buck has carried me through the bumps and bruises of life. Buck was the first true horseman who validated the instincts and feelings that I had been suppressing for so many years. After reading *The Faraway Horses,* I knew that Buck and I had shared some common beginnings. The sensitivity in myself that I had regarded as a painful weakness was the very reason that I resonated with troubled horses—and with people, for that matter. I could put my instincts to use. I didn't have to feel inadequate around other horse people because I refused to implement harsh training techniques. I had a respected trainer like Buck to serve as my mentor, because he was a man and he was gentle.

When my horse Russic developed blindness in one eye, I was overwhelmed by the problem. I referred to Buck's training tapes and Bill Dorrance's book, *True Horsemanship Through Feel*. I knew that the methods of natural horsemanship were going to be our salvation, and I began applying groundwork concepts to my horse. I worked on making him comfortable and trusting. Within four months of consistent and gentle leadership, he made a huge mental recovery. We progressed at his pace, not mine. It was my job to help the horse make it his idea. The second he was overloaded, we reverted to exercises that I knew he could do well. I had no hidden agenda other than to help him make the necessary adjustments. I learned about working under "horse time," and that every day was a new day. I found out how my horse thinks, and learned more about his fluctuating emotional state. I used my eyes and not my mouth. Through Russic's adversity I had found the honest connection that had eluded me for so many years.

Since natural horsemanship was not embraced by the farm where I kept Russic at the time, I had to keep my thoughts and ideas to myself, but I remained steadfast in my commitment to Buck's methods. I imagined a day when all horses could experience the understanding that mine had. I imagined a place and time when the horse would be allowed to express itself. I vowed that one horse and one person at a time, I would convey the message.

Miraculously, Russic's eye did regain full vision. On the darker days of uncertainty I remembered how Buck said it was always darkest before the light. He was right.

Before I encountered Buck Brannaman, I thought that all you did with a horse was ride it. Although I had practiced haltering and done showmanship at local shows, that was the extent of my ground training. And since my horse sensed my fear of lungeing, he obliged my self-fulfilling prophecy by always tearing around at the end of the line like a maniac. I thought that the purpose of lungeing was to take the edge off or to get the bugs out. Today I know differently, and use it as a way to check in with my horse and help him become more focused for the tasks of the day. If we do, however, encounter that extra spurt of energy, I go with it by minimizing my response and actually making it into a game. Instead of the horse seeing this human with pinned-back ears, scowling in fright, he sees a partner who can smile at his strength and physical magnificence. I need to check myself from the perspective of the horse, and I always use my body language and demeanor to help the horse help itself.

Today, I'm very confident with groundwork. I'm able to interpret the horse's every movement, and I enjoy teaching them from this perspective. This is an opportunity to interact through observation and a different kind of contact. I try to know where to stop with each day's lesson. Stop on a good note, and stop when you get a good and honest effort based upon the horse's training level. If it takes ten minutes to get there, then stop at ten and call it a day. I derive as much satisfaction from ground training as I do from riding. I never would have thought this to be possible.

I have methodically sought out clinicians like Mark Rashid, Chris Irwin, and Linda Kohanov. I have garnered their version of humane and sensible horsemanship, while still holding the philosophies of Buck Brannaman close to my heart. Just like Buck, all of them place great importance on using the round pen, a very valuable resource, because an unrestrained horse will function from a totally truthful viewpoint. I know the absolute necessity of making sure that one has a horse's eye in the round pen before ever getting on its back. There is no greater feeling than that experienced when a horse, its head low, slowly and silently approaches you from behind. However, this was not always the case; I have never liked to have a human approach me from behind, let alone a thousand-pound horse. Inside the round pen, I know that my horse is able to listen to me and to keep an ear cocked to the outside world on my behalf. I never tire of seeing a horse hook on and become one with the person on the ground. Knowing the horse would rather be there with me, instead of anywhere else—without a halter or rope to restrict him—is a shining example of how a horse will let a human become part of his life with trust and respect.

At this time, I am pursuing the fundamental principles of equine-assisted psychotherapy with Linda Kohanov of the Epona Equestrian Center in Tucson, Arizona. I have had the pleasure of bringing Linda to Traverse City, Michigan, to share her concept. She has taken the time to observe many herds of horses and to dispel some of the myths that surround them. She has proven over and over that horses are not dumb and stubborn and out to get people. Quite the contrary; she sees that they are very intelligent and highly emotional animals. She says that such high sensitivity is essential to their survival. This parallels the cat/prey/animal theory that Buck shares with us at his clinics.

Through equine experiential learning, I have been able to identify my authentic self and leave that false self outside the round pen, both in dealing with horses and with life in general. I know that I cannot and should not hide my emotions while around a horse, because it drives them crazy when a handler does not maneuver around in accordance with how they feel. Horses are tweaked to sense any incongruity because in the wild, their survival depends on it. And to me, this is a relief. I never wanted to get the better of a horse. It's not our right to dull them or to suppress them; they are not our servants. Only they truly know best how to do lateral work, or how to move their hindquarters. We need to let them go, let them perform for us as best they can given their body conformation. We need to ride our horses in the discipline that is most natural to them. A horse with a natural propensity toward Western pleasure would be subject to physical and mental trauma on the par course circuit for instance. By recognizing our false intentions ahead of time, we will not push a horse into a resistance mode.

My horse Russic was rescued from the Arabian horse show circuit. Although he could surely win in any of the classes they offer, I don't necessarily agree with the way the horses are treated. Of course, there are no absolutes in the horse show world, any more than there are in other areas of riding, but the horses often have quite a bit of pressure put on them, and many don't deal well with that kind of stress.

Today, I ride without a bit, a tie-down, a martingale, or spurs, and I surely avoid using gimmicks. My only goal with Russic is to keep learning from him. He is nineteen years old and has some aches and pains. If I listen, he'll tell me when it's a riding day and when it's a day to just hang together, or we might join his pasture mates and play a long game of Mother May I. Either way, I'm in the presence of the most magnificent, intelligent species God has ever created, and it's all good. I simply close my eyes and recapture my lost childhood. I feel gratitude toward my horse for granting me the opportunity to just be me.

My horse and I are now at a farm that has lots of breeds, many different disciplines, and no pretenses because it isn't a show barn. New riding and training ideologies like Buck's are welcome and appreciated. I know that what I've learned is making a difference for horses and humans alike. I believe that many of life's problems can be solved while in the presence of a horse. My horse allows me to sort things out, and keeps me on task. He will mirror any mental shift and tell me when my assumptions are correct and when they are false. I do believe that my chestnut Arab, with the star, snip, and stripe, chose me.

Buck showed me the importance of becoming a partner to my horse, and taught both of us the value in releasing life's past traumas. He has helped me believe in the wisdom of the horse, and he methodically guides me through the sharing of this message, one horse and one human at a time. Because all creatures on the planet have a responsibility to each other, we are not separate entities but a part of the whole, and I have learned the importance of working with nature, rather than against her.

Finally, I now think more like a horse. I'm able to see the big picture while maintaining a grasp of what is close at hand. I no longer stumble through a life dictated by critical voices from the past. Buck tells us that we cannot move forward if we harbor the resentments of the past. This means a shift from a biased, black-and-white outlook on life. Now I try to view situations from a muted, gray perspective. As an added bonus, every day is touched by the certainty of colorful flecks of hope. For the first time, I know what it's like to be free of self-doubt. The keys to a meaningful existence lie within my own heart and soul. The search for outside approval is over, and all the voices from the past are finally silenced. I have waited a very long time, but my journey has offered me many gifts that I plan to share.

CHAPTER 12

REBELLION AND RECOVERY

This is not the last story, or the last word. They simply go on, and more happens with each person—and horse—I meet. Bill and I chose this story because it involves a father and son, and a family. It's a story that truly touches our hearts, and, we hope, will help you believe.

I met Shayne Jackson in 1995 in Seattle. A masonry contractor, he was interested in riding, and owned Tennessee Walking Horses. Earlier in his life he'd been in Twin Falls, Idaho, ranching a little bit, doing some farming, and working as a bricklayer. When he eventually moved to Washington State, Shayne took lessons with Greg, a man who used to work for me, which is where he learned about the vaquero style of horsemanship.

Shayne ended up going to my clinics when Greg held them in the Seattle area. We became friends, and it became clear to me that Shayne was the type of individual who approached his career with the same zest and vigor that I did. He became incredibly successful in the masonry business, and acquired the nickname "Turbo Man" because he approached everything at a hundred miles an hour, with absolute reckless abandon and no consideration that he would do anything but succeed.

Shayne became a very dedicated student to this style of vaquero horsemanship. I could tell him to practice something, and there was never a doubt in my mind that he was going to approach it with concentrated effort and try. And because he's a smart guy and very coordinated, he's able to adapt to things rather quickly. I longed for the day when he would eventually get rid of his old sour horses that were nothing but trouble for him, and get on a horse that had no baggage. He did end up getting some pretty good horses to ride, and the next thing I knew, not only had he gone beyond being your average backyard horse owner or horseman—he became interested in the craft of becoming a good cowboy.

Shayne owned a small piece of property in Montana that he eventually expanded into a very successful guest ranch, a place where people ride horses with vaquero-style horsemanship. And he's gotten to be a whale of a cowboy himself.

As our friendship grew over the years, I learned more and more about Shayne personally. It was funny how our lives paralleled in a lot of ways. We're about the same age. Shayne married a beautiful lady named Joann who is eight years older than him, just as my wife Mary is eight years older than me.

Joann had two adopted children when they got married, and Mary, my wife, had two children of her own.

Mary's children were wonderful, squared-away young ladies right from the very beginning, but Joann and Shane had their share of struggles with theirs, doing the best they could with what they knew at the time. Yet little did they know, the learning process was really at the beginning, not at the end, about the time we all became acquainted. We saw Shane and Joann become wise beyond their years in terms of how they approach people and how they approach their own kids.

It's hard to share intimate things about your life. Some that I've shared with you are things that frankly could make me feel a little ashamed or a little embarrassed. You want your dad to be someone you're proud of—there's nothing greater than for a boy to brag about his father and think that he's the greatest man in the world. I never had that luxury, but then again, not everybody does. But at the same time, to be able to share of yourself and not worry about what everybody thinks has given me the courage to open myself up to relationships with people I never knew I'd meet, people that share a common thread with myself, like Shane and Joann, who have become our friends.

The story of Shane and Joann and their kids, C. J. and Summer, is a story of victory over incredible, all-consuming obstacles. It shows how a parent can deal with the pain and trouble that kids get into, and how, as a parent, you grow as a person and come out on the other side. Shane and Joann are now enjoying, for the first time in their lives, a family that is what they had always hoped it would be. Their lessons were learned from being around horses, but beyond that by learning how to approach things in a way that's not just fitting for the horse, but also fitting when it comes to dealing with family, and the love they all have for each other.

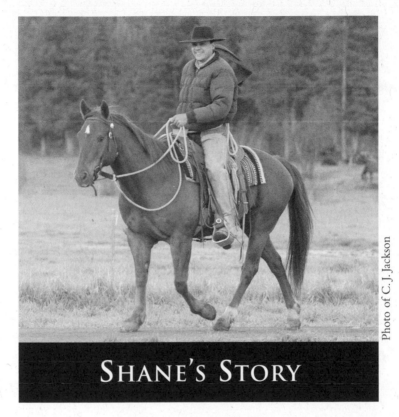

SHANE'S STORY

I never thought that someday I'd be forty-four years old and reflecting back over my life, thinking about what an influence and impression that friends and horses can make in your life.

I started riding when I was about six years old. My mom was an avid horse person. When she was younger, she'd pull all of her hair up in her hat and ride in the men's posse; the guys were always farming or doing other work, and so the posse was always short a few men. It didn't matter what else was going on; Mom could find time to ride no matter how hard she worked. When my brother and I were little, we had a big ole Tennessee Walking Horse named Myrtle. My mom made us little outfits, and we rode in all the parades in Jerome and Twin Falls where we grew up.

As we got older, we rode on ranches, particularly the Clarks' Three Crick Ranch. That's really where I got into cowboying. We kept our horses out there and rode on about forty thousand acres of some of the most beautiful country in the Idaho–Jarbidge, Nevada, breaks. Spectacular country. Growing up riding horses, I never knew much about horse-manship. We just rode them.

At age eleven my parents bought me a mare named Huckan. She bucked me off, breaking my arm and almost my neck. *I've had enough of this,* I told myself. I decided to quit horses and get into dirt bike racing instead. So I quit for a few years (and crashed quite a few times racing dirt bikes). When I was about sixteen or seventeen, I decided to get back into riding horses. It's an odd time in a young guy's life to say, all of the sudden, Okay, I'm not riding motorcycles—I'm going back to riding horses full-time.

So I bought a couple of horses and worked out a place of my own when I graduated from high school. I got to ride quite a little bit up in the mountains, riding out on the Three Crick Ranch whenever possible.

I was twenty years old when I married Leslie, my high school sweetheart (or at least, I thought she was my high school sweetheart at the time). We both had horses, and we enjoyed riding together. In fact, we took a horseback vacation on our honeymoon up Stanley Basin. But that relationship didn't last long, and a year later we found ourselves single again. Leslie didn't have a place to take her horse, so I found myself with one more at my place. With a couple of buddies who also enjoyed riding, I started raising cattle. A good friend of mine, Ralph Wilder in Eagle, Idaho, kind of taught me the business. I'd buy yearling bulls, and would turn them into steers. I also had a hay business, and started custom farming along with being a bricklayer.

After my divorce from Leslie, I worked for Jim Mikesell as a bricklayer. I started as a hod carrier, working my way up to a bricklayer, and then bricklayer foreman. That's when I met Jim's beautiful daughter, Joann. She was recently divorced and had two children, C. J. and Summer, from her previous marriage. They had both been adopted as infants. Joann and I took a liking to each other soon after we met. She's eight years older than me, and had these two kids that their father wasn't interested in raising. We fell in love and married, and for the next few years Joann worked for a law firm in Boise, while we farmed four hundred acres and raised Springer Holstein heifer cattle. I also started falling in love with the kids, and they decided as they got a little bit older—maybe five or six years old—that they'd like me to adopt them. We went to court, and they became mine.

For the next five or six years we farmed and Joann worked full-time at the law firm. By the time our son, C. J., was seven, he could feed a hundred head of cattle almost by himself. And he'd have to, because I was often out of town running big brick jobs around the Boise-Twin Falls area. I was also working out of town with my custom farming. I don't think we ever took a day off, but we loved what we were doing.

That's the way the next few years went, until I decided maybe it was time to consider getting out of the masonry business. I was tired of traveling, of running all over. I kept my hay and my farming businesses going, and I went to college at Boise State for about a year and a half, studying pre-veterinary medicine. I decided to sit out a semester— really the end of my college career—when the guy I had been working for in masonry went broke. Instead of getting out of masonry, I started my own business, a really tough go.

During this time my daughter Summer was doing great. She's one of those children who is just easy to raise. However, for reasons we didn't know at the time, C. J. started to have a lot of problems. He was eight or nine years old when he started running into a lot of trouble at school. Joann and I thought his behavioral issues might have been caused by the anger he felt toward his previous father. We really didn't know what to do.

A counselor met with Joann and me, and then with C. J. We had meetings for quite a while, and he asked me one day, "Have you ever thought that maybe you're doing too much? You're working so hard, and thinking too much about all these jobs. You don't have enough time for your family." I said, "But my family doesn't suffer from it. We all do everything to-gether." He replied, "Well, it may be too much."

I went home that night and I said to Joann, "I'm done. I'm done farming. I'm going to sell everything. I'm just going to stay with the masonry business. We're moving to town." The kids weren't happy because they loved being out on the farm, but we moved to town. Within four months I'd auctioned off all my equipment and sold my cattle and all my crops.

I was just doing the masonry business, and at the time, I felt that was the answer. If I had been putting too much of a burden on my family, I was going to change it. Being a positive person, I just felt the only way out was to make a change. I also told myself that if I ever got back into the horses and the cattle, it would be because I didn't have to do it for a living—I would do it because I loved it. When you love doing something like that, it never leaves your heart. You just have to redirect and dream that someday you may be able to get back to it, whether it works out to be a reality, or just a dream that you still talk about when you're ninety.

In spite of my cutting back, the problems with C. J. escalated. He became suicidal when he was ten or eleven years old. We had to put him in a hospital where he received psychiatric care, but we still couldn't figure out what was wrong. There was one clue, however. When C. J. was younger, he had spent two weeks with his previous dad, against Joann's and my wishes. When he came back, he got out of the car, walked up to me, and slugged me in the stomach. That from a little boy who had never been anything but sweet and kind. I said, "C. J., what was that about? You don't treat people like that." He just had this look in his eye. Then I saw that his hands were burned. He said he was helping his dad do some masonry work, and he had burned his hands on hot rebar. C. J. was never quite the same again, but you don't put two and two together; you just go on thinking everything is fine.

We ended up leaving Boise and moving to Pendleton, Oregon, for a couple of years. C. J. kept getting into trouble. We had him in public and private schools, even in a private school in Hawaii. He got kicked out of there, which is pretty hard to do, but he managed. Everywhere he'd go, he'd do real well at the beginning of the year, but then things would just fall off. Eventually, he started running away from junior high and early high school. We'd get him back, he'd stay for a while, but then he'd be gone again. Finally, he took off with his friends. We know now that at that time he was heavily into heroin. He was shooting up when he was fifteen years old.

Being a parent is one of the most difficult things you can do in this world. And it consumes you when you've been through such things with a child. People will say, "Well, golly, we didn't even know"—but you don't talk to everybody about these kind of things. You keep them inside of you, things you and your wife talk about in the evenings and cry about all the time. And then eventually, you just block it out because you know you have to get tough, just to survive.

The biggest thing about addiction is that you can tell all the right stories; you're pretty darn good at covering your trail. C. J. could smooth-talk his parents into just about any-thing, especially his mother. I was a little more harsh because of being in construction all those years. I'd been around a lot of people who had drug or alcohol addictions; it was easier for me than it was for Joann, who came from a religious back-ground where you just didn't see those kind of things. But anyway, C. J. left and then came back when he was around seventeen or eighteen. He'd been in and out of jail and in other trouble, and now he wanted to start over. He went to work in Seattle with J & S Masonry, and he actually did quite well as an apprentice bricklayer. He could have been a foreman if he had gone on.

In the interim, Joann and I bought a ranch in Montana. Our dream of getting back to ranching because we loved it, not because we had to, was becoming a reality. I bought some horses, because you can't have all this country and cattle and everything and not have horses. It wasn't because my first horse was a Tennessee Walking Horse, but I simply ended up buying Walkers as they presented themselves. And that was the beginning of my total life change. It came from meeting Buck Brannaman.

When I found I was having trouble with one horse, and couldn't quite get through to him, I pulled out the Yellow Pages. I called a number under "Natural Horsemanship," and met Greg and rode with him. I heard Buck Brannaman was coming to Ellensburg. Greg told me he was one heck of a horseman, so I packed my gear and signed up for his February clinic.

Joann and I had never seen a man who could work horses like that. It was absolutely beyond anything you could imagine. We ended up going to dinner with Buck that night. We had so much in common: married before, a wife eight years older, kids from a previous marriage. From this first meeting, a friendship was born.

I signed up for every Brannaman clinic I possibly could. All of a sudden, I had a total life change, enabling me to enjoy horses. Mine were tough; not really bronc-y enough to buck you off, not the typical kind that got yanked and pulled on until their eyes were about to blow out of their head, but still, they needed some work. So with the bit of knowledge I had, I worked with them. Joann and I bought a nice acreage in North Bend, and I rode every day, or I'd be out there at night under the lights.

C. J. came back home and actually took a little interest in the horses for maybe a couple of weeks, but that was about it. He was starting to slide again. We were sitting at the table one night and I said, "You're back on the drugs, aren't you?" C. J. denied and argued, and Joann said we were picking on him when Summer, who was taking a psychology class in college that covered addiction, ran through all the symptoms with C. J. right then and there. He continued to deny, but the fact of the matter was, he knew that we knew. The next day he packed up and took off in his truck, gone again.

He was out of our lives for quite a while. We didn't have any idea whether he was dead or alive. He'd call every three or four months—he'd be back in jail, and he'd say he wanted to change his life and he was ready, but it was always when he was in jail, and wanted us to bail him out. We told him we might help him, but only when he got out—that he needed to stay the course. If he got in trouble with the law, our philosophy was simple: You do the crime, you do your time.

Joann and I continued to sign up for every Brannaman clinic we could ride in, traveling all over to ride with Buck. As far as I was concerned, I was going to be the best student Buck Brannaman had ever seen. And it wasn't just about horses; it was a way of life, the way that you interacted with people and horses. What I loved about the horses is, you were on an even playing field. It didn't matter whether you were a doctor, lawyer, professional golfer, or a model. That horse didn't care who you were or what you did. It's what you had to offer him, and that realization changed my life forever.

What happened over the next few years really laid it all out. I'd mentioned to Buck that if he ever had a horse come up for sale, I'd sure like to buy a nice ranch gelding. And he said, "I might have a couple." I did want to make my own, too, but when you can buy something that Buck Brannaman's put a handle on, there is nothing that equals it in the world.

I met Rawlin, Buck's foster sister's husband, at one of the clinics. He invited me to ride with him. I was pretty intimidated about roping, because even though I could rope, there are so many good hands out there. So I practiced every spare hour of the day. I rode and roped until my arm ached, and then I roped some more. I quit all my other hobbies, sold my snowmobiles, and quit softball, tennis, and golf so I could ride horses.

When Joann and I were on vacation in Guadalajara with the Brannamans, Buck and I were sitting by the fireplace, relaxing and smoking cigars. We were talking about doing what you love to do in life as your job. Buck said, "Well, you know, I've been fortunate. Every day of my life I'm doing exactly what I love to do." I said, "I love what the masonry business has given me, but I can't tell you that it's what I love to do every day. I want to do what I love to do."

I came back from that trip thinking about how I could spend the rest of my life with horses. I thought about it over the next year, and came up with this idea of starting a guest ranch where you do this style of vaquero horsemanship. There were a lot of doubting Thomases, but the only person who honestly believed in me was Buck Brannaman.

Joann and I bought the ranch across the way from our place and started building the whole facility. I asked Rawlin to help me, and he and I went to a horse sale where I bought eighteen head. He and I started riding every one of them. I hired a young man from Wyoming, and we all rode my horses. I mean, we rode hard, five to eight horses every day. We started riding in March as the snow was coming off. The buildings were all done that spring, so about August, I told Rawlin that I was going to advertise. I expected just a few guests so we could get the butterflies out before really opening the following year, but we ended up booking sixty-eight guests. The ranch was a huge hit. Almost all the people came back the next year. The first full year we had more than two hundred guests. Now, we have 70 percent repeats.

C. J. had been in more trouble and had spent some serious time in jail, all drug and alcohol related. He wasn't a bad kid; he just couldn't get away from drugs. One day we got a phone call that he was back in jail again, but this time Joann and I and Joann's folks helped him out. C. J. did pretty well for a while, working with a contractor that I knew down in Idaho. It looked like he was starting his life over, but soon, he was in trouble again and ended up back in jail. That was the cycle: in jail, out of jail, on drugs, back in jail, dry up, back out, on drugs. It didn't look like things would ever change—but you go on hoping.

The guest ranch was going great, and our other businesses were too. People told me that I was changing. My nickname before used to be Turbo Man, because no dust settled on my shoes. Rawlin used to look at me and say he had never seen anybody that could go like I can go. But all of a sudden, things started fitting. I rode around on my horses with a big smile on my face. It was like the horse was teaching me something. The part that is the most intriguing to me is that when you have that opportunity to learn from an animal as noble as a horse, it changes your life forever. I was living it, riding with my guests, sharing the knowledge that Buck had taught me.

I always hoped that someday I might be able to share this with my son, but the possibility seemed remote. If I was on the Pacific, he dang-sure was on an island somewhere out in the Atlantic—and he had a lot of shark-infested waters to swim through to get back to where we'd ever be together again. As far as C. J. was concerned, I didn't see any light at the end of the tunnel. Every time the phone rang, I was sure it would be the last call I'd ever get, and someone would say, Your son's gone because of the drugs that he's shooting up. Sooner or later, that's the way it would end.

In December, 2002, C. J. called out of the blue and said, "Dad, I'm out of jail again. I'm doing great. I'm staying out of trouble, staying off the drugs. I've got a new life. My girlfriend's pregnant. We're going to have a baby, and you're going to be grandparents. I just wanted to let you know that we're doing great." I said, "I hope that you plan on growing up and taking care of your child, because now you've got a lot more responsibility in life than just satisfying your own needs." And he said, "This time, it's different."

It wasn't. A while later his girlfriend called to say C. J. was back in jail, on a probation violation for possession of drug paraphernalia. He called, wanting me to bail him out, but I told him I wasn't going to help him; he needed to do his time, which was six months.

But C. J. went to the judge and asked if he could go to rehab, to a place in Gooding, Idaho, called the Walker Center, a fabulous facility with a good success rate. The judge agreed, and C. J went there to start rehab. While he was there he met Mike Lanthony, his counselor, who started working with C. J., prying into his head and trying to find out what happened in his life to cause him so much trouble.

And it all came out. Joann got a phone call one day that C. J. had talked, and there was a problem. As we might have suspected, when C. J. was a child, he had been treated horribly by his previous father. That's why he had gotten so far into drugs and alcohol; they were the only way he knew how to hide from it.

It was a hard thing for Joann and me to deal with. Joann, who had been married to the guy, was devastated. She wanted to get even with her ex-husband and make him pay, force him to make it right. I wanted to find a way for C. J., now with that weight off of his shoulders, to move forward and have a better life. Joann and I struggled with that, back and forth. It was a real tough time for us.

C. J. and I began to patch up our relationship. He called me from the Walker Center, and I called him. We talked one or two and even three times a day. I hired an attorney to help. C. J. had gone back to the judge to ask if he could stay longer in the Walker Center; he was given another month to six weeks. We continued to talk a lot. He said he wanted to get out of there and come to Montana. I knew he could never go back into the construction world with my company, because that environment would be deadly; he'd soon be back in trouble again. But I did say that I had a place for him—at the ranch. Horses would be a neat thing in his life.

C. J.'s going to the ranch, riding horses, being a cowboy, and learning something from the horses would be a pretty substantial change in life from baggy pants, a do-rag on his head, partying, drugs, and living for the moment—completely opposite from the direction his life had taken. But out of desperation more than anything, he was ready for a change.

In the interim, he decided he didn't want to marry the woman who was having his child. The child is a beautiful girl named Vanessa, and C. J. stays very involved with her.

C. J. finished at the Walker Center, then went back to jail to finish the rest of his sentence. He called me one day and cried, "Dad, I hate this place." I replied, "Well, you should hate it, son, but you've got to spend your time to get out of there so you can be here at the ranch." And every day I'd tell him about the ranch, and what was going on.

When C. J. got out of jail, I found him a job in Idaho to see how he'd cope with the world. This time, he seemed to be doing fine, so Joann and I went to pick him up and bring him to the ranch. We didn't say much on the way home; there wasn't much to say. He had a lot to absorb. I looked over at him, sitting and looking out the truck window as we drove through Montana. I'll never forget it. He had the look of a deer caught in the headlights. He looked down that road like he was looking at reality—I'm going to Montana to be a cowboy, whatever that means. Don't get me wrong. C. J. enjoyed being around the horses before, but it was always short-lived. The drugs always had a bigger hold on him than anything else.

We stopped by a store and C. J. bought a few pairs of Wranglers and some cowboy boots. I'd already ordered him a pair of custom boots to ride in, and we headed for the ranch. C. J. knew he had to start riding and interacting with the guests and learning about this new way of life.

He had read Buck's book, *The Faraway Horses,* and realized he wasn't alone in what his life had been, but that he had a new lease on life. During the week he'd be in his cowboy gear and off riding, and on weekends he'd wear his do-rag and baggy pants. Being cowboys, the staff razzed him a little bit, but they took him under their wing. C. J. took the razzing okay, and started seeing the light pretty quick. For the first time in his life, his self-esteem was coming up, because people who came to the ranch took one look at this six-foot-five cowboy and thought he was pretty cool.

C. J. really wanted this life. He put his heart in it. He rode hard, and every day I watched him and thought, *This is amazing.* And I'd talk to him about horses. We'd sit around for hours and I'd just tell him what an opportunity he had to learn from the horse, how much it had changed me. He told me, "Dad, you've changed so much it's just unreal; the way you address issues and you don't really yell anymore, and you always seem to find a solution."

I said, "If you just open your eyes, the horse has a way to talk to you and teach you about a lot of things. You don't have to use words. He'll just teach you." And so C. J. and I rode, and we laughed, and he got better and better. Friends from Seattle who knew him from his earlier life visited, and they said they couldn't believe how far C. J. had come, riding around in pressed shirts and having fun. His self-esteem was the biggest benefit. For the first time in his life, C. J. felt like he was somebody. And he was. He had a goal—to be a good horseman— and he set out to accomplish that goal. I don't know if I've ever seen anybody come so far, so fast, in just a year's time. He can rope, he can ride, he sits a horse beautifully. He's still got a lot learn, but like he says, "Dad, it's the horses."

I'll never forget the day C. J. said, "Dad, the lessons that I'm learning come from the horses. When you think you have a problem or something, you get on a horse, and you find help. I can't even believe it's me. It's the least amount of money I've ever made in my life and the happiest I've ever been. You don't need money when you have this, and the horses . . ." He smiled at me before he want on. "Dad, no matter what's going on in your day, when you're out there riding and punching cows or taking guests out riding or teaching them about horsemanship in the arena, every day is a new experience."

It's been about a year and a half now. C. J. has stayed off drugs and alcohol. His probation officer (he's not completely released) is in awe of how great he's done. The other day someone asked him, "C. J., what are you going to do in the future? What do you see your future holding?"

He answered, "You're looking at what I'm going to be doing for the rest of my life. I'm living where I'm going to die. This ranch is everything to me, and all I have to do now is learn how to get there. Through all the stuff that the horses have shown me, I do see the light now, and I do see how I'd like to be."

We were riding out the other day and I watched C. J. loping across the meadow ahead of me, and I just got this smile on my face. How lucky I am to have had the chance to give my son this opportunity. It isn't about the ranch or anything else; it's really about having the opportunity to see him survive. I know in my heart that if it wasn't for where I'm at today and what I've experienced—learning from the horses that there was a way out for C. J.—he probably wouldn't be alive today. He'd be the first to tell you he was on the edge. All I had to do was offer the chance to C. J., and then help him succeed.

Now I see him interacting with the guests and their horses, enjoying this way of life, and I see guests come back and say how much C. J. has changed and how well he's doing. Like C. J. says, "It's like riding a horse, Dad; you just take it one day at a time and use the lessons of yesterday. It's a new beginning today, and every day it's the same for me as it is for the horse. What it was yesterday was yesterday, and what it is today is what I have to offer. And that's where I'm at in my life."

As for Joann, she has the opportunity to see somebody each day that she once believed was lost forever. Now, he's a big part of our lives, and it's special beyond words. I've tried to put it in words and it's extremely difficult. All I know is that when people say, "You seem so happy, and we've never seen your horses look better," I just smile and think what a lesson this has all been. I am the luckiest man in the world because of the horses, and the rewards they have given me and my family.

AFTERWORD

I've devoted my life to improving the world of the horses and people I meet and work with. The lessons I've learned along the way are near and dear to my heart, and I've done my best to pass them on to others who might need some direction in their lives. The stories in this book help me feel I'm on the right track.

Multitudes of people seem interested in what I have to offer and the ideas I'm trying to teach. It's very gratifying to see so many new folks coming out of the woodwork to hear what I have to say, even though there was a time when I couldn't get arrested with this stuff. However, through it all, my faith in and dedication to what I do has never wavered.

I read somewhere a very profound statement: "The excellence in every art consists in the complete accomplishment of its purpose." Over the years I've come across plenty of people who criticized me because they subscribed to the old-school methods of dominating a horse. They worked a horse as if they were going to war with it. And they were. If that's the way you deal with your horses, it's the way you deal with your fellow man as well. I just can't subscribe to that primitive notion of forcing your will on a horse or a human, and I hope if nothing else, this message comes through for my readers.

When I was young and just starting out with horses, a fellow shared something written by Teddy Roosevelt. I've

found it to be a great response to people who expected me to
fail in my endeavors. I'll leave you with those words:

> *It is not the critic who counts, not the man who points
> out how the strong man stumbled, or where the doer of deeds
> could have done them better. The credit belongs to the man
> who is actually in the arena; whose face is marred by the dust
> and sweat and blood; who strives valiantly; who errs and
> comes short again and again; who knows the great enthu-
> siasms, the great devotions, and spends himself in a worthy
> cause; who, at the best, knows in the end the triumph of high
> achievement; and who, at worst, if he fails, at least fails while
> daring greatly, so that his place shall never be with those cold
> and timid souls who know neither victory nor defeat.*

And so my journey continues, friends, working toward the
complete accomplishment of my purpose. That's the excellence in the art form I've chosen. I hope our paths cross.
Good luck on your journey. Be well, my friends, and always
believe—in your horses and yourselves.